PROFITABILITY THINKING

Simple Concepts, Strategies and Tools to
Effectively Manage Cash Flow and
Make More Profitable Business Decisions

———————

John Bulman, MBA

ISBN-10:   0985098503
ISBN-13:   978-0-9850985-0-6

Light bulb image © istockphoto.com/bulmanjohn
Cover design by Rosa Barnes

Printed in USA

Dedication

This book is dedicated to my wife, Lupita, who insisted I do what I always said I wanted to do. That is, to write a book. Saying that I want to do something new and actually doing it are two different things. Sometimes it takes a bit of loving support to start the fingers typing and keep them typing until the job is done.

Lupita's belief that writing this book is part of what I need to do to live a full life and realize my potential was an inspiration that kept me going. Sometimes it takes someone close to you to see clearly what is only an apparition to you.

Thank you and I love you.

Acknowledgements

I want to thank Alan Ahr, Mike Calabrese, Larry Keen, Ralph Turner and others for making Profitability Thinking a better book. Your input was offered out of friendship and was extremely valuable in improving the quality of the book.

I also want to thank Rosa Barnes, who found a way to translate my thoughts into a book cover that is really beautiful.

Table of Contents

Table of Contents Details

.

Chapter 1
Introduction
Read Me First

"I want to understand my financials." I've heard some version of this statement over and over from managers and business owners. What I've come to realize is that these business owners and managers didn't so much want to learn how to understand their financials as how to USE them to manage their businesses more effectively. They wanted to know how to use the metrics generated by their businesses to show them where their profits, cash flow and business risk were coming from, what these numbers meant and what to do about them.

With this book, I've tried to create a system for basic financial understanding, and then to assemble a group of concepts, strategies and tools to help business owners and managers to use those skills. That is, to help business people run their businesses more profitably, with less risk and with better cash management. Other topics covered will include business planning, key performance indicators and profitable personal activity management. All of this information presented in a compact, easy to understand format that busy business people will be able to use efficiently to change their approach to managing their businesses and engage in what I like to call Profitability Thinking.

Numbers Matter

When I was a teenager, there was a couple with whom my parents were friends. He was a manufacturer's representative for a number of relatively small manufacturing companies. At one point, one of these manufacturing companies was for sale and they decided that this was their opportunity to grab the brass ring. To make real the dream of a business of their own. To provide a better life for their family. From what I understand, they mortgaged their house and depleted their savings to acquire this business, and have some working capital to run it. They also bought the company just as the economy was going into a recession.

This couple dropped out of sight. They weren't attending parties or neighborhood events because they didn't have time. They didn't even attend a couples bowling league because that was an extra expense and there was no money for extra expenses. It all went into the business. Even with the long hours and saving every penny, the business came close to going under taking their house, their savings and their dream with it. But by watching the business's finances with a close eye toward cash flow, profitability and efficiently using every resource the company had, they saved the business.

As it turned out, the company survived and prospered. The couple not only saved their business and their house, but bought a large new house and two others as vacation homes from the profits of what was then a flourishing business. It truly was an American success story.

It's not unusual for a small business such as theirs to find itself in a fight for financial survival at some point in its existence. For many small businesses and start up businesses, it's not if they will be in financial jeopardy at some point, but when.

Although my parents friend's company survived and prospered, it almost didn't. That would have made it part of the 51% of businesses that, according to the SBA, fail in their first five years. The biggest reason these businesses failed was that they were undercapitalized. They ran out of cash. Their numbers didn't work. So the entrepreneur's aspirations, money and time invested disappeared. In many cases they didn't even know their numbers weren't working and were running their businesses blindly. The numbers matter.

> The quantitative aspects of the business matter.
> The internal measurements of the business matter.
> Understanding the financial statements of the business and what those numbers mean, where the numbers came from, and what processes drove them matters.
> Reading the financial statements and internal financial reporting monthly, at a minimum, matters.
> Understanding the profit impact of pricing and marketing decisions matters.
> Understanding which customers and products are profitable and which are not matters.
> Understanding the balance sheet ratios that measure risk and effectiveness matters.
> Knowing how to budget and manage cash flow matters.
> Knowing how to manage time and resources effectively matters.

These and many other numbers matter because getting them right minimizes the chance that your business will find itself in a fight for financial survival and maximizes the chance it will survive one. Getting the numbers right protects your dream and your money, and can provide you and your family with a better life. When your business, your business activities, your products and your customers are profitable, your life gets better.

To which I hear you say, "so what!" "All that's as obvious as the ocean being blue and the sun rising in the east." Am I right? I hope so. It is obvious. My point was to get agreement that the quantitative aspects of the business are important, and that understanding them so you can manage them is essential to a successful and profitable business. I will cover all of the above points in this book.

Why I Wrote This Book

The problem is that many business owners and managers don't clearly understand what's important when it comes to measuring the performance aspects of their business, that is to say the numbers. They don't understand the metrics that if managed to, would make them more money. Perhaps you find yourself among those who would like to know more but don't know where to begin. You are extremely busy and these skills seem inaccessible, and also seem to take a lot of additional time and mental energy that you simply don't have.

That's why I wrote this book. To make measuring the performance of your business easy to understand and accessible. To provide information that is simple, practical and easy to implement. To introduce you to concepts, strategies and tools that you can understand quickly and start using immediately to manage your business more profitably, predictably and effectively. Managing to key metrics will help your business become more profitable, make your cash flow more predictable and your business activities more effective.

The Problem with Traditional Financial Education to Business Owners and Non-Financial Managers

I have taught finance and profitability to business managers who had P&L responsibility in three companies and I've always been amazed at what I have found. Very smart and educated people who were experts in their field but knew very little about what made their businesses profitable. And they wanted to learn. But like many business owners, these managers found their financials overwhelming and not particularly helpful in making business decisions. They were experts in another business discipline (typically sales and marketing), were very busy and so they learned the absolute minimum to get by, even when part of their compensation was tied to their business unit's profitability. There was always something more urgent to attend to and like learning a new language, it took them out of their comfort zone.

The problem with most books and other educational products that attempt to provide financial and quantitative information to business owners and managers is that it is taught as finance. It looks like finance. It sounds like finance. And it provides a well rounded background in finance. All important information that never gets read and so never gets used. I know because I have provided this kind of information in the past and it didn't help my audiences.

A number of years ago, I was presenting financial education to a small group of managers. I'm a numbers geek, so I was excited about the financial material I was presenting. Basically I was showing my audience what the numbers on their financial statements meant. At the end of my presentation, one of the managers asked, "So how does this help me run my business?" I thought it was self evident, but it wasn't. What I needed to explain was what the numbers meant, where these metrics came from, what processes created them and how they might be improved. Then I needed to give them tools outside of their financial statements that were more useful. That would have helped this manager and the others in the room to run their businesses better. I haven't forgotten that episode and that manager's question is one of the questions I have asked as I have created this book. The others being:

> ➤ Do they need to know this?
> ➤ Can this be easily implemented?
> ➤ How can I make this simpler and easier to understand?

I hope you find this book useful. It is intended to give you tools to help you be more effective at managing your business so that it can be more profitable with predictable cash flow and less business risk. The information presented is meant to help you with your goal of business success by changing your thinking about your business and your approach to managing it. That is the beginning of Profitability Thinking.

What is Profitability Thinking?

Profitability Thinking is a systematized way of thinking about your business and business activities that allows you to develop strategies to be more effective at running your business. It is knowing your numbers so that you can make better decisions that lead to greater profitability and having the tools to do so. It's doing a little math upfront so you know whether your decisions will help your profitability and what the impact on cash flow will be.

To aid in this process, we must end the confusion of your financial statements. More importantly, we need to identify ways you can use the metrics from your business to create different tools and reports that address specific aspects of the business, allowing you to manage your business and business activities more effectively. At the end of this book you will have an understanding of some concepts and strategies to make your business more profitable and manage your cash flow more effectively, as well as the tools to support those concepts and strategies. You won't know everything about the finances of your business, but you will know enough to make an impact and make better decisions. You will be engaged in Profitability Thinking.

You will need to ask your accountant or a very good bookkeeper to create some of the reporting presented in this book for you, although much of the reporting is fairly simple to assemble if you have your basic financial information. This may cost you a little more money which at first you might not be willing to spend, as you might not want to add another administrative expense to your fixed costs. My advice is to spend the money or the time to make this happen. The small added expense pales in comparison to the potential cost of mispricing your products and services, making an unprofitable investment in facilities and equipment, or missing a troublesome expense or cash flow trend because you were operating with insufficient information.

Using this Book Effectively

As an undergraduate student, I was in an economics class that used a textbook created by some merciful author who put a summary of each chapter at the beginning of the chapter. It was a couple of pages long and it covered the basics of that chapter's subject. There wasn't a lot of detail and if you didn't understand some of the basic concepts, you did need to read the chapter. However, if you had enough knowledge in combination with the summary to understand the contents of the chapter, it saved you from having to read the whole chapter. I have used this concept in the creation of this book.

What you will find is that chapters 2 through 9 will have a pre-chapter summary that covers the basic information presented in that chapter. If you fully understand the information presented in the summary, you won't need to read the entire chapter. There is also a glossary presented in chapter 14 that will cover various concepts presented in the book, and can be used to supplement the pre-chapter summaries as well as a reference to which you can return after you've finished the book. The glossary will be in alphabetical order for easy reference.

Following the pre-chapter summary, the entirety of that chapter's information will be presented in traditional chapter format, complete with examples elaborating on the concepts, with exercises in the back of the chapter should you wish to practice using the information. I recommend doing the exercises as they will help you retain what you have learned. For answers to the exercises, go to **www.profitabilitythinking.com**.

As you read through the chapters, you will have ideas about how to use the information in your business. At the end of the chapters there are notes pages to provide you with a convenient place to capture your ideas.

There will also be tools provided in Excel format to help you with some of the concepts, such as a break even calculator and cash flow budget template. You can find these tools at **www.profitabilitythinking.com**. The chapter will point you to the website whenever information is covered where there is a tool available.

By formatting the book in this way, I have tried to provide you with a learning environment that is efficient to your purposes and skill level, whatever they may be. The point is to give you the information you require without having to read additional information which you might not find as useful. Let's begin.

Chapter 2
Very Short Finance Basics
Pre-Chapter Summary

1. This chapter includes:
- ➤ Accrual accounting and cash accounting - profit is not the same as cash
- ➤ Financial statement basics
- ➤ A basic introduction to the Income Statement
- ➤ A basic introduction to the Balance Sheet
- ➤ A basic introduction to the Cash Flow Statement
- ➤ A basic introduction to the aged receivables and payables reports
- ➤ A note about accountants and financial statements

2. Cash accounting recognizes revenue when cash (an accountants term for immediately spendable assets such as physical cash, checks, money in unrestricted bank accounts, funds transfers, etc) is received and recognizes an expense when an obligation such as a bill is paid. Accrual accounting recognizes revenue when goods are shipped or a service provided, and recognizes an expense when the business sells a product or takes on the obligation to pay for something. Because of this, in accrual accounting profit does not necessarily equal cash.

3. The financial statements are generated by the accounting system. For every transaction there are at least two entries entered into the accounting system that affect either an income statement account - revenue or expenses, or a balance sheet account - assets, liabilities or owner's equity.

4. The three basic financial statements are:
- ➤ The Income Statement or P&L (Profit and Loss)
- ➤ The Balance Sheet
- ➤ The Statement of Cash Flows

5. The income statement contains revenue and expenses, and answers the question, did my business make a profit? Did my revenue exceed my expenses for a specific period of time, typically a month, a quarter or a year.

6. The balance sheet shows the financial condition of your business at a specific point in time. The components of a balance sheet are assets, liabilities and owner's equity.

7. The statement of cash flows shows the sources and uses of cash in your business. It shows changes in cash from:
> ➢ Operations
> ➢ Investment Activities
> ➢ Financing Activities

8. The formula for cash flow is:

Profit
+ Depreciation/Amortization (cash from operations) (add back non-cash expense)
± Inventory change (cash from operations) (inventory increase means cash decrease)
± Accounts Receivable change (cash from operations) (accounts receivable increase means cash decrease)
± Accounts Payable change (cash from operations) (accounts payable increase means cash increase)
± Fixed Asset change (cash from investing activities) (fixed asset increase means cash decrease)
± Debt Obligations (cash from financing activities) (debt increase means cash increase)
= Cash Flow

9. The accounts receivable aging report shows the age of your receivables and whether your customers are paying per the terms agreed to.

10. The accounts payable aging report shows you how many bills are coming due, for what amount and if your suppliers are being paid.

11. In this book, you will be exposed to various ways to create financial information that are extremely useful to your efforts to manage your business. Getting your accountant or a very good bookkeeper to create this information is part of the process, although much the information is fairly simple to assemble if you have your basic financial information.

12. At a minimum, the three basic financial reports should be reviewed monthly, and the aged receivables and payables reports reviewed weekly.

Chapter 2
Very Short Finance Basics
Profitability Thinking Has to Start Somewhere

This book provides easy to understand and easy to implement concepts, strategies and tools that you can use immediately to manage your business more effectively and profitably. It's not meant to provide a complete and well rounded background in finance, although there is certainly value in that as well. However, the ideas presented in this book have much of their basis in finance and so a quick review of finance basics will minimize any confusion as we proceed. We'll start with a few accounting basics. Other topics covered in this chapter include the differences between cash and accrual accounting, the concept that cash does not necessarily equal profit, a brief introduction to the three basic financial statements, and an introduction to the aged receivables and payables reports.

The material covered in this chapter is intended to introduce you to various reports and concepts. In other words, to show you that they exist and provide a little bit of information about them. This chapter's material is not all the information that will be presented in this book about them. There are three chapters about the income statement, breakeven analysis and profit projection, and how to use them; two chapters about the balance sheet, and ratios to determine business risk and the financial health of your business; and two chapters about cash flow management that include the statement of cash flows, cash flow budgeting, the aged receivables and aged payables reports, and 50+ ways to improve cash flow.

Accrual Accounting and Cash Accounting
Profit is Not the Same as Cash

There are two types of accounting: cash accounting and accrual accounting. With the exception of one person personal service businesses and small cash based businesses, accrual accounting is better than cash accounting because it reflects the economic reality of the business. Cash accounting recognizes revenue when cash (an accountants term for immediately spendable assets such as physical cash, checks, money in unrestricted bank accounts, funds transfers, etc) is received and recognizes an expense when an obligation such as a bill is paid. Accrual accounting recognizes revenue when goods are shipped or a service provided, and recognizes an expense when the business sells a product or takes on the obligation to pay for something. The problem with cash accounting is that it has the potential to be misleading in terms of how your business is doing.

As an example, Maria has a small service business that uses cash accounting and sells her services to large companies. When she performs work for her customers, she submits an invoice to the accounts payable department in those companies for the work done. Because she uses cash accounting, she records revenue when she receives a check from those companies, sometimes as much as 45 days later.

Maria did a lot of work for one customer in April along with her regular flow of business from her other customers. In fact, she had an outstanding month in April because of the onetime increase in business from the one customer on top of her normal business. However, she had a poor February and March, so she didn't collect much cash in April for the business she did in those months. She did collect a record amount of cash in May from the large amount of work she did in April, even though the amount of work she did in May was only average.

So which was Maria's great month; April when she did the work or May when she collected the cash? Maria is a one person service business, so this time shift doesn't pose a significant management problem.

Now it's two years later and Maria's business has grown. She now has 10 people doing the work she used to do and is selling products as well as services. Maria is now managing a much more complex business, and needs to know when sales are made and when expenses actually happen. She needs to be able to track projects, collect milestone payments, and match her expenses with the work performed and products sold. Can you see where using cash accounting might create difficulties understanding what is going on in her business?

Most businesses use accrual accounting to better reflect the reality of their business. As previously stated, this method of accounting records revenue when the product is shipped or service performed, records the cost of goods sold when the product ships and not when it's made, and records an expense when the business assumes the obligation to pay for something. The implication is that profit does not necessarily equal cash received. All examples in this book will use accrual accounting.

In the case of Maria's business, accrual accounting will allow her to record revenue when her business sells a product or performs a service, and recognize expenses when products are sold, or goods and services for the business are purchased and not when they are actually paid for. This "reality" accounting presents Maria with a much more accurate picture of her business.

The issue for Maria then becomes, how does she keep track of cash? There are a number of ways to do this including looking at her statement of cash flows and using a cash flow budget.

The profit does not equal cash aspect of accrual accounting means that a business not only has to know that it is profitable, but also needs to know what its cash flow situation is at any point in time. In the chapters that follow, I will cover simple ways to understand if your business is profitable in any given scenario, as well as go through strategies to manage your cash flow. Many profitable businesses have failed because they didn't manage cash flow and had all of their cash tied up in un-spendable assets such as inventory and accounts receivable. You can't spend profits, you can only spend cash. You need to manage both cash and profitability.

Financial Statement Basics

The financial statements are generated by the accounting system. For every transaction there are at least two entries recorded in the accounting system that affect either an income statement account - revenue or expenses, or a balance sheet account - assets, liabilities or owner's equity. Asset and expense accounts are increased by a debit entry on the left hand side of a transaction record and decreased by a credit entry on the right hand side of a transaction record. Liabilities, owner's equity and revenue are increased by a credit entry on the right hand side of a transaction record and decreased by a debit entry on the left hand side of a transaction record.

To show you what I mean, let's look at an example of a $1,000 product sale on credit, or terms.

Journal Entry for Sale of Product

	Debit	Credit
Sales revenue		1,000
Accounts receivable	1,000	
Inventory		447
Cost of goods sold	447	
Sale of goods		

As you can see, the revenue account is credited $1,000 for the sale and the accounts receivable asset account is debited for the same $1,000, while the inventory asset account is credited $447 to reflect the reduction in the value of the inventory and the cost of goods sold expense account is debited $447 to reflect the cost of the goods sold in the transaction. The gross margin on the sale is $553 or 55.3%, which reflects the $1,000 sale amount minus the $447 cost of goods sold. At this point there is no increase or decrease in cash.

When the cash is finally received 30 days later, the entry would look like this:

Journal Entry for Receipt of Payment

	Debit	Credit
Cash	1,000	
Accounts receivable		1,000
Receipt of payment		

All of the transactions in the period such as those in the example are recorded in a journal, and then tallied in separate accounts such as the ones used in the transactions above to keep running balances. When it comes time to generate the financial statements, these various accounts are combined to produce the three basic financial statements, which are:

➢ The Income Statement or P&L (Profit and Loss)
➢ The Balance Sheet
➢ The Statement of Cash Flows

These financial statements, and a number of ancillary reports which I will also cover, are the mechanism of keeping track of your business and they are interconnected. That is, information from one flows into the other.

Knowing how to analyze financial statements allows you to use them to your advantage. There is information which can be gleaned directly from these statements, but also from other reports that can be generated from the data used to create these statements. Some of the things you can do with the information are:

➢ Compare the current financial performance of your business in key areas with its previous financial performance to identify favorable and unfavorable trends so you can manage them.
➢ Develop and manage key business ratios that indicate the financial health and risk of your business so that investors and lenders will view the business favorably.
➢ Know the point at which your business or a product breaks even, which is key to understanding the viability of business initiatives.
➢ Create projections simulating various business conditions involving pricing, marketing, sales volume and fixed costs so you can make the most profitable business decisions, and avoid wasting money and opportunities.
➢ Create a cash management strategy and simple cash flow budget to always be on top of your cash situation and avoid unpleasant cash flow surprises.

As you can see, knowing how to use your business's financial reports and other business metrics has real value. Let's start with a basic overview of the three primary financial reports as well as the aged receivables and payables reports. All will be covered in greater detail, including how to use them, later in the book.

The Income Statement

The income statement answers the question, did my business make a profit? Did my revenue exceed my expenses for a specific period of time, typically a month, a quarter or a year. It will capture sales revenue, cost of goods sold (which are the costs directly associated with the production of the goods that were sold), fixed operating expenses, interest expense and tax expense, if applicable. <u>It does not show whether cash increased or decreased.</u> The next three chapters will cover the income statement in some detail, as well as introduce you to breakeven analysis and profit modeling. These tools will allow you to spot trends, show the amount of sales your business will need to break even, and explain how to project future profits at various levels of sales, contribution margin percent and fixed costs.

Using the income statement and related tools to make better pricing, product, customer and investment decisions should improve your business's profitability.

The following is an example of an income statement formatted in the traditional way:

Traditional Income Statement

XYZ Company		
P&L Report for Month Ended May 31		
Gross Sales	89,106	
Sales Returns and Allowances	(4,000)	
Sales Revenue	85,106	
Cost of Goods Sold	38,000	44.7%
Gross Margin	47,106	55.3%
Operating Expenses		
Salaries, Wages and Commissions	17,000	20.0%
Benefits and Taxes	4,000	4.7%
Office Expense	1,000	1.2%
Rent, Utilities and Services	12,000	14.1%
Sales, Marketing and Advertising	6,000	7.1%
Depreciation	1,106	1.3%
Other Expenses	4,000	4.7%
Total Operating Expenses	45,106	53.0%
Operating Profit	2,000	2.4%
Interest expense	2,000	
Net Income / Profit	0	0.0%

The Balance Sheet

If the income statement shows your business's profitability over a period of time, then the balance sheet shows the financial condition of your business at a specific point in time. The components of a balance sheet are assets, liabilities and owner's equity. Assets are then broken down into current assets and fixed assets, and liabilities can be broken down into current liabilities and long term liabilities. Owner's equity is what's left when you subtract liabilities from assets.

The formulas for the balance sheet are

Assets - Liabilities = Owner's Equity
or
Assets = Liabilities + Owner's Equity.

Because the balance sheet is a snapshot in time of your business's financial condition, you can use that information to develop ratios which point to the financial health and risk of the business. There will be two chapters about the components of the balance sheet, and more importantly, how to develop and use ratios to determine your business's financial health.

Profitability Thinking

An example of a ratio that can be developed from balance sheet information is the current ratio, which is the ratio of current assets to current liabilities and measures your business's liquidity, that is its ability to pay its bills. There are other ratios that measure investment in receivables and inventory, and ratios measuring the ability to service debt. All very useful indicators to manage cash flow and business risk that are easy to understand and identify, and the kind of information lenders look at to make decisions about investing in your company.

What follows is an example of a balance sheet:

Balance Sheet

XYZ Company	
Balance Sheet for Year Ended December 31	
Assets	
Current Assets	
Cash and Equivalents	75,000
Accounts Receivable	125,000
Inventory	150,000
Prepaid Expenses	20,000
Notes Receivable	5,000
Other Current Assets	25,000
Total Current Assets	**400,000**
Fixed Assets	
Land	100,000
Buildings	150,000
Machinery and Equipment	100,000
Capitalized Leases	50,000
Leasehold Improvements	25,000
Furniture and Fixtures	50,000
(Less Accumulated Depreciation)	(150,000)
Deferred Costs	20,000
Other Fixed Assets	20,000
Total Fixed Assets	**365,000**
Total Assets	**765,000**
Liabilities	
Current Liabilities	
Accounts Payable	100,000
Notes Payable	35,000
Current Income Taxes Payable	10,000
Wages Payable	15,000
Accrued Liabilities	10,000
Current Portion of Long-Term Debt	30,000
Other Short-Term Liabilities	20,000
Total Current Liabilities	**220,000**
Long-Term Liabilities	
Non-current Long Term Debt	300,000
Deferred Income Taxes	15,000
Notes Payable to Officers and Owners	10,000
Other Long-Term Liabilities	50,000
Total Long-Term Liabilities	**375,000**
Total Liabilities	**595,000**
Equity	
Preferred and Common Stock	120,000
Retained Earnings	50,000
Total Equity	**170,000**
Total Liabilities and Equity	**765,000**

The Statement of Cash Flows

The statement of cash flows shows the sources and uses of cash in your business. It shows changes in cash from:

> ➢ Operations
> ➢ Investment Activities
> ➢ Financing Activities

Cash from operations starts with your business's profit and then adds back non-cash expenses such as depreciation and amortization, as well as changes in receivables, payables and inventories. Changes in cash from operations may be a source of cash or use of cash. Cash from investment activities typically has to do with your company's investment in facilities, plant and equipment, and is generally a use of cash. Cash from financing activities is about the assumption and repayment of debt as well as payment of dividends, and stock sales and repurchases, and can be a source or a use of cash.

Sources of cash can be operations, new loans, issuing stock or sale of plant and equipment. Uses of cash can be operations, dividends, loan repayment, stock repurchase or purchase of plant and equipment.

The formula for cash flow is:

> **Profit**
> + **Depreciation/Amortization (cash from operations) (add back non-cash expense)**
> ± **Inventory change (cash from operations) (inventory increase means cash decrease)**
> ± **Accounts Receivable change (cash from operations) (accounts receivable increase means cash decrease)**
> ± **Accounts Payable change (cash from operations) (accounts payable increase means cash increase)**
> ± **Fixed Asset change (cash from investing activities) (fixed asset increase means cash decrease)**
> ± **Debt Obligations (cash from financing activities) (debt increase means cash increase)**
> = **Cash Flow**

If you look at it in its entirety, the cash flow statement can be the most confusing of the three basic financial statements to understand. For that reason, in the two chapters about cash flow and cash flow management, I'm going to zero in on a few key basics you need to know and useful strategies for how to improve your cash flow. These will include tips for accounts receivable, accounts payable, inventory and expense management, as well as how to put together a simple cash flow budget so you can always be in control of your cash situation.

Below is an example of a statement of cash flows:

Statement of Cash Flows

XYZ Company		
Statement of Cash Flows for Period Ending December 31		
Cash Flow from Operations		
Net Income from Income Statement	196,800	
Accounts Receivable Increase	(50,000)	
Inventory Increase	(10,000)	
Accounts Payable Increase	20,000	
Prepaid Expense Increase	(5,000)	
Depreciation	13,272	
Net Cash Flow from Operations		**165,072**
Cash Flow from Investing Activities		
Equipment Purchase	(10,000)	
Net Cash Flow from Investing Activities		**(10,000)**
Cash Flow from Financing Activities		
Increase in Long-Term Debt	50,000	
Net Cash Flow from Financing Activities		**50,000**
Net Increase (Decrease) in Cash		**205,072**
Cash at the Beginning of the Period		**75,000**
Cash at the End of the Period		**280,072**

What we have just covered was an introduction to the three basic financial statements. I recommend that you read and analyze these three reports monthly, at a minimum.

There are two more reports that I would also like to introduce you to, which are the accounts receivable aging report and the accounts payable aging report. These two reports should be read weekly to see where your business stands when it comes to collecting from customers and paying suppliers. I will present more about these two reports in the chapters about cash flow management.

Aged Receivables and Aged Payables Reports

If your business offers its customers credit terms to purchase your product or service, then keeping track of how old your accounts receivable balances are is essential to managing your cash flow and collecting the money owed to you. The accounts receivable aging report shows the age of your receivables and whether your customers are paying per the terms agreed to. Below is an example of an accounts receivable aging report.

Accounts Receivable Aging Report

XYZ Company Accounts Receivable Aging Report							
Customer	0-10 Days	11-30 Days	31-60 Days	61-90 Days	91-120 Days	> 120 Days	Total
ABC Corp	5,000	5,000		2,000			12,000
DEF Corp	-	15,000	5,000				20,000
GHI Corp	5,000						5,000
JKL Corp	-	25,000		3,000			28,000
MNO Corp					5,000	5,000	10,000
PQR Corp	5,000	5,000		10,000			20,000
STU Corp		25,000	5,000				30,000
Total	15,000	75,000	10,000	15,000	5,000	5,000	125,000
Percent of Total	12.0%	60.0%	8.0%	12.0%	4.0%	4.0%	100.0%

Similar in form to the accounts receivable aging report is the accounts payable aging report. Just as you expect your customers to pay you on time, your suppliers expect to be paid on time as well. However, you have to manage your cash to be able to do so. One way to do this is by reviewing an accounts payable aging report. This will show you how many bills are coming due, for what amount and if your suppliers are being paid. The following is an example of an accounts payable aging report.

Accounts Payable Aging Report

XYZ Company Accounts Payable Aging Report					
Supplier	**0-10 Days**	**11-30 Days**	**31-60 Days**	**> 60 Days**	**Total**
ABC Corp	5,000	5,000			10,000
DEF Corp	-	15,000		5,000	20,000
GHI Corp	5,000				5,000
JKL Corp	-	25,000			25,000
MNO Corp	5,000				5,000
PQR Corp	5,000	5,000			10,000
STU Corp		25,000		5,000	30,000
Total	**20,000**	**75,000**		**10,000**	**105,000**
Percent of Total	**19.0%**	**71.4%**		**9.5%**	**100.0%**

A Note About Accountants and Financial Statements

Finding the right accountant can improve your chances for business success. Accountants vary greatly in experience, expertise, the services they provide and fees. Here are some tips about hiring an accountant that's right for your business.

> ➢ You can find an accountant the way you would any other supplier. Ask for referrals, do research, interview several prospective accountants, check their fees for the work you require and check references.
> ➢ Find an accountant who has prior experience in your industry. Such experience can be of great benefit to you as your accountant can advise you from a background of experience in the business you are in.
> ➢ Find an accountant that you're comfortable with and one who is willing listen to you. This will be an ongoing relationship and your accountant should be your trusted advisor.
> ➢ A CPA is more expensive than a general accountant. For audits and loan applications, a CPA may be necessary. For monthly or quarterly information, the expense of a CPA may not be necessary, and a general accountant or good bookkeeper might be a more appropriate choice.
> ➢ Try to find an accounting firm that matches your business's size. If you're a small business, find a small accounting firm that will give you the attention you're looking for.

Give this some thought and some effort. Picking the right accountant will pay ongoing dividends. Picking the wrong accountant will make it more difficult to achieve your financial and business goals.

Often it seems that accountants only create financial statements for other accountants or the government. They create the information necessary to meet the requirements for publishing a set of financial statements or to file your taxes, but these financial statements really tell you very little. They lack detail or are formatted in a way that doesn't provide the information you need to run your business.

In this book, you will be exposed to various ways to create financial information that are extremely useful to your efforts to manage your business. Getting your accountant or a very good bookkeeper to create this information is part of the process. If your accountant won't create this information, you might consider finding an accountant who will or learn how to create this information yourself. It's worth the extra money or time to create this information because you will be able to make more profitable and more cash efficient decisions that are worth far more than the relatively small amount of time or expense involved.

Summary

Knowing your financial statements and what can be done with them can help you:

> ➤ Make better decisions that improve your profitability
> ➤ Improve your cash flow
> ➤ Reduce your risk

At a minimum, the three basic financial reports should be reviewed monthly, and the aged receivables and payable reports reviewed weekly.

From the data used to create the three basic financial reports, other tools such as breakeven analysis, profitability projections and financial ratios can be created, aiding in the development of strategies to improve cash flow and profitability.

Finally, the numbers in their various forms can be used to develop strategies for pricing, marketing, capacity management, staffing, business planning and budgeting. The numbers can also be used for things you won't see on financial reports such as opportunity costs and activity effectiveness. We'll explore these as well.

Notes

_____

_____

_____

_____

_____

_____

_____

_____

_____

_____

_____

_____

_____

_____

_____

_____

_____

Chapter 3
The Income Statement and Profitability Improvement
Pre-Chapter Summary

1. This chapter includes:
   - The contents of the Income Statement
   - The Income Statement for service businesses
   - Spotting trends in the Income Statement
   - Profitability ratios
   - 13 ways to improve profitability
   - Introducing the breakeven formatted Income Statement

2. The contents of the income statement include:
   - Gross sales
   - Sales revenue which is gross sales minus returns and allowances
   - Cost of goods sold which is direct materials and direct labor (COGS)
   - Gross profit which is sales revenue minus cost of goods sold
   - Operating expenses not related to COGS, interest or taxes
   - Operating income (loss)
   - Interest expense
   - Pre-tax income (loss)
   - Taxes
   - Net income (loss)

3. The income statement for a business that only sells services does not have a cost of goods sold, since no products are sold. Most costs fall into the operating expense category.

4. If the income statement is detailed enough, it can be used to spot trends by comparing a series of income statements from consecutive time periods. Spotting trends is one way of using your business's metrics to manage your business better.

5. Gross margin percentage is calculated as
   Gross Profit / Sales = Gross Profit Margin Percentage.
   Operating profit percentage is calculated as
   Operating Profit / Sales = Operating Profit Percentage.
   Percentage of operating expenses to sales is calculated as
   Operating Expenses / Sales = Percentage of Operating Expenses to Sales.
   Net income percentage is calculated as
   Net Income / Sales = Net Income Percentage.

6. There are 13 ways to improve profitability presented in this chapter. Not every strategy will fit every business, but take a look and see if there are things you can implement today.

7. PROFITABILITY THINKING
> ➢ Make a commitment to read all of your financial statements including your income statement monthly with an eye toward finding improvement opportunities.
> ➢ Have your accountant or a very good bookkeeper create income statements for your business that show multiple units of time side by side. Make sure these income statements have enough line item detail, as well as profitability ratios and fixed cost items as a percent of sales to provide the information necessary to identify trends in your business that can be managed.
> ➢ Create profit improvement opportunities by spotting trends in your business. This seems simple, but are you doing it on a regular basis?
> ➢ Develop plans to manage each area identified and take action. The whole point of creating and reviewing this information is to create improvements to your business based on what the information reveals.
> ➢ Based on your review of your income statement, what was the trend in:
>> o Returns and allowances?
>> o Cost of goods sold/gross profit as a percent of sales?
>> o Total operating expenses and various individual operating expenses in absolute terms as well as in percent of sales?
>> o Operating profit and net income percentages?
> ➢ What are your plans to address issues discovered?
> ➢ Review the 13 ways to improve profitability presented in this chapter and see if any of them could be implemented today.

8. What are your business's metrics for the last three months in the areas listed below? Do you see any trends developing?

Gross margin percent of sales - _____ _____ _____

Operating profit percent of sales - _____ _____ _____

Fixed cost percent of sales - _____ _____ _____

Net income percent of sales - _____ _____ _____

Chapter 3
The Income Statement and Profitability Improvement
Measuring Profitability Thinking

The income statement is a summary of transactions over a specific accounting period, typically a month, a quarter or a year. It's also commonly referred to as the P&L (Profit and Loss). Essentially it is revenue minus expenses equals a profit or a loss. Again, profit does not equal cash. Revenue is recognized when a sale is made, which may be on credit, or terms. For sales on terms, cash is collected later when your customer pays the invoice. When product is manufactured or merchandise for resale is purchased and put into inventory, it is not recognized as cost of goods sold expense until the product or merchandise is sold. Products and merchandise put into inventory are charged to accounts payable, and cash is paid later when the payable is due. As you can see, revenue and expenses are not the same as cash inflow and cash outflow, hence profit does not equal cash.

What follows is an example of what an income statement in the traditional form looks like. When your accountant or bookkeeper creates your income statement, it is essential that they provide at least the level of line item detail appropriate to your business that is similar to the one below. This will help you identify manageable performance metrics for your business. The very basic income statement format of revenue minus SG&A (selling, general and administrative) equals operating profit doesn't have enough information. Following the income statement example is an explanation of each of the line items in the example income statement.

In this book, I will not cover tax expenses and our examples going forward will stop at pre-tax income, and pre-tax income will be net income in future income statement examples.

Traditional Income Statement

XYZ Company		
P&L Report for Month Ended May 31		
Gross Sales	89,106	
Sales Returns and Allowances	(4,000)	
Sales Revenue	85,106	
Cost of Goods Sold	38,000	44.7%
Gross Margin	47,106	55.3%
Operating Expenses		
Salaries, Wages and Commissions	17,000	20.0%
Benefits and Taxes	4,000	4.7%
Office Expense	1,000	1.2%
Rent, Utilities and Services	12,000	14.1%
Sales, Marketing and Advertising	6,000	7.1%
Depreciation	1,106	1.3%
Other Expenses	4,000	4.7%
Total Operating Expenses	45,106	53.0%
Operating Profit	2,000	2.4%
Interest expense	2,000	
Net Income / Profit	0	0.0%

The Contents of the Income Statement

Information contained in the income statement might include the following, and can include more.

- Gross Sales - Total sales revenue during the period.
  - (Sales returns and allowances) - Credit given for items returned and discounts granted.
- Sales Revenue - Sales revenue after subtracting returns and allowances (Sales).
- Cost of Goods Sold - Direct costs incurred in the production of products for sale that were sold during the period or the purchase cost of merchandise that was sold during the period. In manufacturing, these costs are direct labor, direct materials and may include an allocation of manufacturing overhead such as quality control or production planning. Cost of goods sold is how manufacturing costs and purchase costs of merchandise for sale are recognized, and are not recognized until a product is sold. Costs that went into the manufacture of product or purchase of merchandise for sale are recognized as inventory until product sale and then are cost of goods sold expense.
- Gross Profit - Sales for the period minus cost of goods sold for the period. When gross profit is expressed as a percentage of sales, it's called Gross Margin.
- Operating Expenses - Expenses incurred during the period in the operation of the business that are not directly related to cost of goods sold. These would include salaries, wages, commissions, benefits, payroll taxes, rent, office expense, sales, marketing, depreciation and other expenses.
  - Salaries, Wages and Commissions - The pay of employees not directly involved in the production of products to be sold.
  - Benefits and Taxes - Costs of benefits provided to employees such as health insurance, and taxes such as Social Security, Medicare and unemployment insurance.
  - Office Expense - The cost of running an office including supplies and minor pieces of equipment.
  - Rent, Services and Utilities - Rent paid for the use of facilities, utilities, and services such as janitorial and security.
  - Sales, Marketing and Promotions - Expenses incurred for advertising, trade shows, samples and demonstration products, and other costs involved in trying to increase sales.
  - Depreciation Expense - Reduction in the value of capitalized plant and equipment during the period as part of the scheduled depreciation of these items over a period of time.
  - Other Expense - Expenses that don't neatly fit into any of the other listed expense categories. If a component of the other expense category is large, create a new category for that major expense.
- Total Operating Expenses - The sum of the operating expenses listed above.
- Income (Loss) from Operations - The gross profit for the period minus total operating expenses for the period.
- Interest Expense - Interest paid or accrued during the period on long term and short term debt obligations.
- Pretax Income (Loss) - Income from operations for the period minus interest expense for the period. For LLCs and S corporations, this is the bottom line as taxes on the business income are typically paid as part of the owner's personal income taxes. Consult your tax advisor or attorney for more information.
- Income Taxes - Federal, state and local income taxes paid or accrued during the period on pretax income for that period.
- Net Income (Loss) - Pretax income for the period minus income tax expense for the period. This is the bottom line.

The Income Statement for Service Businesses

The income statements for service businesses look very similar to income statements for businesses that sell products except that they don't have a cost of goods sold expense (provided they don't sell products along with the service) and consequently don't have a gross margin. Most of the costs associated with a business that sells only services are operating expenses, typically the salaries, wages and benefits of the people who work for the business. Below is an example of what a typical service business income statement looks like.

Traditional Income Statement for Service Business

XYZ Company		
P&L Report for Month Ended May 31		
Gross Sales	85,106	
Sales Returns and Allowances	-	
Sales Revenue	85,106	
Cost of Goods Sold	-	0.0%
Gross Margin	-	0.0%
Operating Expenses		
Salaries, Wages and Commissions	49,000	57.6%
Benefits and Taxes	10,000	11.8%
Office Expense	1,000	1.2%
Rent, Utilities and Services	12,000	14.1%
Sales, Marketing and Advertising	6,000	7.1%
Depreciation	1,106	1.3%
Other Expenses	4,000	4.7%
Total Operating Expenses	83,106	97.6%
Operating Profit	2,000	2.4%
Interest expense	2,000	2.4%
Net Income / Profit	0	0.0%

Spotting Trends in the Income Statement

Income statements can also be constructed to facilitate their side by side comparison over sequential periods of time. Besides comparing the actual numbers over time, it can also be helpful if you compare percentages such as percent of cost of goods sold to sales revenue (sales), gross profit to sales or operating costs to sales. These ratios can be very useful in determining how your business is trending.

Profitability Thinking

Below is an income statement showing three consecutive months. Notice the trends in the various line items and the percentages associated with them.

Three Month Trend Income Statement

XYZ Company						
P&L's for the Months of April through June	April		May		June	
Gross Sales	63,000		89,106		125,000	
Sales Returns and Allowances	(3,000)	-4.8%	(4,000)	-4.5%	(5,000)	-4.0%
Sales Revenue	60,000		85,106		120,000	
Cost of Goods Sold	26,790	44.7%	38,000	44.7%	53,580	44.7%
Gross Margin	33,210	55.4%	47,106	55.3%	66,420	55.4%
Operating Expenses						
Salaries, Wages and Commissions	15,904	25.2%	17,000	19.1%	18,614	14.9%
Benefits and Taxes	3,500	5.6%	4,000	4.5%	4,300	3.4%
Office Expense	1,000	1.6%	1,000	1.1%	1,000	0.8%
Rent, Utilities and Services	12,000	19.0%	12,000	13.5%	12,000	9.6%
Sales, Marketing and Advertising	6,000	9.5%	6,000	6.7%	6,000	4.8%
Depreciation	1,106	1.8%	1,106	1.2%	1,106	0.9%
Other Expenses	3,500	5.6%	4,000	4.5%	5,000	4.0%
Total Operating Expenses	43,010	68.3%	45,106	50.6%	48,020	38.4%
Operating Profit	(9,800)	-15.6%	2,000	2.2%	18,400	14.7%
Interest expense	2,000		2,000		2,000	
Net Income / Profit	(11,800)	-19.7%	0	0.0%	16,400	13.7%

From the above three month income statement, what can you determine about this business? Here are a few things I noticed:

> Gross sales increased dramatically over the three months, almost doubling, while sales revenue actually did double during the period.
> Sales returns and allowances decreased from 4.8% of gross sales to 4% of gross sales.

- The cost of goods sold and gross margin percentages stayed constant at 44.7% and 55.4% respectively, however gross profits doubled. Having a stable cost of goods sold and gross margin percent is fairly normal over a three month period, although maintaining a stable cost of goods sold and gross margin percent in a situation where sales doubled in a short period of time is noteworthy. More about the stability of gross margin percent and fixed costs within ranges of business activity will be covered in the next chapter.
- Fixed costs increased over the three months in absolute terms, but declined as a percentage of sales as sales growth exceeded fixed cost growth by a wide margin. This is operating leverage. If you can keep fixed costs relatively stable while increasing sales, your profitability improves dramatically.
- Because of maintaining a stable gross margin percentage and keeping fixed costs under control while doubling sales, the business went from a $11,800 monthly loss to a $16,400 monthly profit in three months.

As you can see, there are trends in the previous example that need to be explained and managed. Why did sales double? Why did returns and allowances decline as a percent of gross sales? How was the gross margin maintained? How were fixed costs managed and is there an area for improvement? It might be very useful to you to have your accountant or bookkeeper create income statements in this format so you can see the trends in your business and look for ways to influence them. If you already have a series of individual income statements, it's fairly simple to put this information together yourself.

For a three month income statement template and a period over period variance income statement template, please go to www.profitabilitythinking.com.

Profitability Ratios

In the example income statements shown previously, we saw that performance of various aspects of a business's profitability can be measured over time to spot trends that indicate improving results or developing problems. There are other ways to measure your business's profitability from the information in the income statement. These are ratios and percentages comparing one number in the income statement to another number in the income statement. The reason that ratios and percentages are useful is that they put the numbers in context. The gross profit for the month of May shown in the income statement examples was $47,106. Was that good? The only way the number makes sense is to measure it against sales as a percentage, in this case 55.3%. Then you can see if the gross profit is acceptable or not, because it is in context. You can then track the percentage over time to see if your efforts to manage your profitability are having the desired effect.

The ratios below are called profitability ratios. They measure various levels of profit within the income statement to sales.

> Gross margin percentage
> Operating profit percentage
> Net income percentage

Gross margin percentage is calculated as

Gross Profit / Sales = Gross Profit Margin Percentage.

Remember that gross profit is sales minus cost of goods sold. If the percentage to sales is decreasing, it may mean that increases in your costs are outstripping your increases in pricing. So are your costs of production rising because of inefficiency? Are the costs of materials or merchandise you buy increasing, and those cost increases are not being passed through to customers? It could mean that there are opportunities for process improvements, better purchasing or re-pricing of your products.

Operating profit percentage is calculated as

Operating Profit / Sales = Operating Profit Percentage.

You will want to compare the operating profit percentage over time to see if there are improvements or developing problems. Remember that operating profit is calculated as gross profit minus operating expenses. The operating profit percentage has all the same issues as the gross profit percentage, plus the addition of fixed costs into the equation. If the percentage is decreasing, is there a problem with your gross margin? Are your fixed costs getting out of line? Again, you may spot opportunities to improve based on the trending of this percentage.

As an aside, although not strictly a profitability ratio, the **percentage of operating expenses to sales** is a way to keep tabs on the efficiency of your operating expenses. If the percentage is increasing, this may indicate a problem as your fixed costs are increasing at a faster rate than your sales. This percentage can be calculated as

Operating Expenses / Sales = Percentage of Operating Expenses to Sales.

Net income percentage is calculated the same way as the others and tracks your bottom line. Remember that net income is calculated as operating income minus interest expense and taxes (if applicable). So net income percentage is calculated as

Net Income / Sales = Net Income Percentage.

If everything is going as planned through your operating profit percentage, but your net income percentage is decreasing, then the problem lies in the amount of interest you're paying or your taxes.

There are two other profitability ratios that can be calculated using the income statement, but they also require the use of balance sheet information. They are:

> ➢ Return on Assets
> ➢ Return on Equity

I will cover these in the chapter about balance sheet ratios.

13 Ways to Improve Profitability

No chapter about the income statement should end without some ways to improve profitability, so below are 13 ways to improve your profitability. Review them and see if any of these might offer an opportunity to improve the profitability of your business or inspire an idea that could improve your profitability.

> ➢ Improve sales and margins by suggesting related purchases. If you've ever been to a shoe store, bought appliances, been to a restaurant or had your car's oil changed, you know what I'm talking about. Most businesses have related high margin products or services to sell. If you don't, what are some products or services you might consider adding? Related to selling additional high margin items is up selling to a better product or service with a better margin. When you buy a car, perhaps you'd like the model with a navigation system and eight speaker stereo. Finally, have a robust spare parts business. Spare parts are more profitable than new products and can continue sales revenue after the initial sale.
> ➢ Improve your margins by adding more value to your product or service and charge a premium for it. Examples might be improving product quality, enhancing product performance or creating a unique feature, improving service levels, better post sales support, and better product training.
> ➢ Improve your sales and margins by rewarding your sales people for up selling, selling related high margin items and spare parts. Make it worth the sales person's time to feature products and services that do your business the most good.

> ➤ Improve revenue and margins by stopping revenue leaks. Diagram your sales process from taking the order to final collection and find where money is falling through the cracks. Likely causes will be sales not turning in an invoice or customers not being charged for additional work. You might find that your revenue has been leaking out of your business.

> ➤ Improve revenue and margins by raising your prices. If you haven't raised your prices in several years, it's about time to do so. You may have started in business with low prices that you haven't raised even though you don't need to price that aggressively anymore. Evaluate ways to raise prices that cause the least upset with your customers. Related to this is to eliminate or minimize discounting. Test whether discounting is really necessary to make the sale.

> ➤ Improve your gross margin by engaging in value engineering of your products. Is there a less expensive item to substitute, a less expensive process or a lesser tolerance in the manufacturing of the product that would work just as well? Use your suppliers expertise to suggest ways of taking cost out of your products.

> ➤ Improve your gross margin by engaging in ongoing margin analysis and volume analysis for all products as part of your management routine. Reviewing your product lines can highlight which popular or high margin products should be featured with your customers, which products have volume or margin issues that need to be fixed, and which products need to be discontinued.

> ➤ If you have adequate cash on hand, improve your margins and reduce fixed costs by taking the trade discount for paying your invoices early. Taking a 2%, Net 30 trade discount creates an annualized return of approximately 36% on what is in effect a short term loan to your supplier (2%, Net 30 means that the terms of your payable with your supplier allows you to take a 2% discount if you pay in 10 days, or you can pay the full amount in 30 days). If you have adequate cash to take discounts for early payment but your supplier doesn't offer them, consider negotiating for them.

> ➤ Improve revenue and reduce fixed costs by measuring the return on marketing expenses. Did the marketing add enough sales with enough margin to justify the spend? Could it be done differently to produce a greater return next time? Also, use cooperative advertising to reduce your marketing expenses. With co-op advertising, your supplier pays for part of advertising expenses that feature their product. Typically the amount they pay is determined by how much you buy.

- ➤ Decrease fixed costs by requiring senior management approval of employee expense reports and require backup for those expenses. Question everything that doesn't make sense. Also, scrutinize employee mileage reimbursement. If the employees know their expenses are being scrutinized, they will be less likely to try and get reimbursed for inflated expenses.
- ➤ Costs cannot be controlled until they are broken down and quantified. How many hours at what labor rate? What are the material requirements? How many hours per service call? How much time to produce a sale? Improve your gross margin and reduce your fixed costs by breaking down your processes and see if there are efficiencies that can be created.
- ➤ Find the gross profit and operating profit percentages that are appropriate for your industry or business line, and see if your margins are at least as good as the industry average. These metrics can usually be found in data provided by industry associations or industry publications.
- ➤ Be aware of purchases you make because "the business bought it and I can write it off." Just because you can write it off doesn't mean it's free. The government is in effect subsidizing your purchase by your marginal tax rate, but you are still paying real money for the item you purchased. As an example, if your marginal tax rate is 28% and you buy a $1,000 item that you write off, you will receive a $280 reduction in your taxes, but you paid $1,000 for the item. Assuming you expensed the item, you had a net usage in cash of $720. The moral to this story is not to buy things you would not otherwise buy because the business bought it and you can write it off. Consult your tax advisor for guidance on tax issues.

Clearly this list does not contain all of the ways that your business can improve profitability, but I hope you found an item or two that might work in your situation, or at least that reading the list generated an idea of your own that you can try today.

PROFITABILITY THINKING

- ➢ **Make a commitment to read all of your financial statements including your income statement monthly with an eye toward finding improvement opportunities.**
- ➢ **Have your accountant or a very good bookkeeper create income statements for your business that show multiple units of time side by side (ideally sequential months/quarters). Make sure these income statements have enough line item detail, as well as profitability ratios and fixed cost items as a percent of sales to provide the information necessary to identify trends in your business that can be managed. If you already have a series of individual income statements, it's fairly simple to do this yourself.**
- ➢ **Create profitability improvement opportunities by spotting trends in your business. This seems simple, but are you doing it on a regular basis?**
- ➢ **Develop plans to manage each area identified and take action. The whole point of creating and reviewing this information is to create improvements to your business based on what the information reveals.**
- ➢ **Based on your review of your income statement, what was the trend in:**
  - o **Returns and allowances?**
  - o **Cost of goods sold/gross margin as a percent of sales?**
  - o **Total operating expenses and various individual operating expenses in absolute terms as well as in percent of sales?**
  - o **Operating profit and net income percentages?**
- ➢ **What are your plans to address issues discovered?**
- ➢ **Review the 13 ways to improve profitability presented in this chapter and see if any of them could be implemented today.**

The first step in gaining control of your business is having the information necessary to manage it. From the three month income statement example, you can see that if the income statement is detailed enough and it covers multiple units of time, you can spot trends that will lead you to profitable action.

What are Your Business's Metrics?

Since this is a book designed to encourage you to use the information presented, I will have sections throughout that ask you to do some homework. In this case, to use some of the concepts in this chapter as they apply to your business. Please calculate your business's gross margin percentage, operating profit percentage, fixed cost percentage and net income percentage for the last three months? If you have this information, great! If not, please take the opportunity to do so now. Are there any trends developing?

Gross margin percent of sales - _____ _____ _____

Operating profit percent of sales - _____ _____ _____

Fixed cost percent of sales - _____ _____ _____

Net income percent of sales - _____ _____ _____

Introducing the Breakeven Formatted Income Statement

The income statements previously shown tell you if you made a profit or not, and can be used to compare current business performance to previous performance in various revenue and expense categories. In the previous example, the company went from a loss to a profit due to identifiable changes in the performance of the business. But the income statement in its traditional format is not useful for understanding your breakeven point or for creating projections about how your business might perform under a different set of circumstances. Projections such as what your profit would be at different sales levels, what your breakeven point would be with increased overhead, and what the effects to profitability of a price increase / decrease might be.

There is a way to revise the format of the income statement to accomplish these types of projections. The revised report breaks expenses into fixed costs (costs that stay essentially the same regardless of volume) and variable costs (costs that increase and decrease with volume). I call it the breakeven formatted income statement, which is a short hand term I use to describe an income statement that classifies expenses in this way.

The next two chapters are devoted to the breakeven formatted income statement, and how it can be used to find your breakeven point and project profits under various business conditions. I will show you that by manipulating existing information, you can create a tool that that can be used to make management decisions. Please see below an example of a breakeven formatted income statement derived from the information in the traditional income statement example for the month of May shown previously. As you can see, there is a significant difference in the two formats even though the sales, cost of goods sold and profit in the breakeven formatted income statement are the same as in the traditional income statement.

Breakeven Formatted Income Statement

XYZ Company		
P&L Breakeven for Month Ended May 31		
Sales Revenue	**85,106**	
Variable Expenses		
Cost of goods sold	38,000	44.7%
Variable operating costs	7,106	8.3%
Total Variable Expenses	**45,106**	**53.0%**
Contribution Margin	**40,000**	**47.0%**
Fixed Expenses		
Fixed operating costs	38,000	44.7%
Interest expense	2,000	2.4%
Total Fixed Expenses	**40,000**	**47.0%**
Profit	**0**	**0.0%**

Let's see how to use this tool to run your business more effectively and profitably. This is where Profitability Thinking really gets interesting.

Notes

_____

_____

_____

_____

_____

_____

_____

_____

_____

_____

_____

_____

_____

_____

_____

Chapter 4
The Breakeven Point and Profit Projection
Pre-Chapter Summary

1. This chapter includes:
- ➢ Breakeven analysis
- ➢ Income Statement formats
- ➢ Breakeven analysis for service businesses
- ➢ Contribution margin percentage and fixed costs are stable to a point
- ➢ When fixed costs and contribution margins change

2. Breakeven analysis takes information used to create the income statement (P&L) and rearranges it into a different kind of income statement. Its components are sales revenue (sales), variable costs and fixed costs. Sales revenue is revenue after returns and allowances are deducted. When you subtract variable costs from sales you get a contribution margin, which is labeled as such because it is the portion of a sale that contributes to the payment of fixed costs and then to profit.

3. To calculate your breakeven, divide your fixed costs by your contribution margin percent.

Fixed Costs / Contribution Margin percent equals Break Even.

4. The chapter compares the traditional income statement to the breakeven formatted income statement.

5. Breakeven analysis for a service business is calculated the same way as for businesses that sell products, but since there is no COGS, their contribution margin percent is higher. Their costs are mostly fixed and are typically larger as a percent of sales than for businesses that sell products.

6. PROFITABILITY THINKING

> Assist your accountant or bookkeeper in creating a breakeven formatted income statement for your business, as well as for major divisions, product lines or services within your business on a regular basis.

> Calculate your breakeven point and project a likely profitability level reflecting the goals of your current business initiatives using the information provided in this section.

> Knowing your breakeven point and having the ability to project profits under various scenarios will improve your ability to make basic decisions about your business and avoid costly mistakes because you will understand the likely effects of decisions before you make them.

> Make plans to improve your contribution margin by raising prices, reducing the cost of goods sold, reducing variable operating costs or changing the mix of products you sell to focus on the more profitable items.

> Create incentives with your sales people to change your product sales mix by selling more profitable items or up-selling additional profitable items.

7. What are Your Business's Metrics in the following areas?

My business's current monthly sales are: _____

My business's current contribution margin % is: _____

My business's current monthly fixed costs are: _____

My business's current breakeven point is: _____

My business's current monthly profit is: _____

My business's calculated profit projection using breakeven analysis is:

_____

8. Contribution margin percentages and fixed costs don't generally change in the short run. However, they are predicated on a range of volumes similar to your recent, normal business operations. If you operate dramatically outside of that range, your cost structure may change and you will need to take that into consideration by changing your breakeven calculations and possibly your management decisions.

Chapter 4
The Breakeven Point and Profit Projection
Profitability Thinking Starts With Profits

One of the limitations of the basic financial statements is that they don't lend themselves easily to decision making. So there are other tools that use the information from the financial statements, as well as other quantitative data derived from company operations, to create more usable decision making tools. Two of these are the breakeven formatted income statement and breakeven analysis.

The breakeven format for income statements is not new, but it's not part of the financial statements normally supplied by accountants or finance departments. Although most of the managers I have worked with in various businesses could understand their bottom line and a few individual line items in their traditional income statements, they couldn't see if the individual strategies to manage their business units such as pricing, marketing and staffing were working. What most managers saw was a sea of numbers. I introduced them to a way of measuring the effectiveness of their actions managing their business units and how their business decisions might perform under a variety of circumstances. The tools I used were the breakeven formatted income statement and breakeven analysis.

I used to teach managers breakeven analysis from a presentation I created entitled "Does Your Financial Model Work?" I taught these managers to easily see if what they were doing to manage their businesses was going to lead them to their desired profitability levels. I wanted them to be able to make basic business decisions with a general idea of what the outcome would be. To give these managers tools that would allow them to roughly project on the first day of the month what their profit would be at the end of the month.

Breakeven Analysis

Breakeven analysis takes information used to create the income statement (P&L) and rearranges it into a different kind of income statement. Its components are sales revenue (sales), variable costs and fixed costs. Sales revenue is revenue after returns and allowances are deducted. Revenue can be for products sold, services performed, or commissions and bonuses received.

Variable costs are costs associated with the production and sale of products or services that increase or decrease with volume such as cost of goods sold (direct labor and materials), sales commissions paid, delivery charges, sales bonuses paid, and direct supplies. All of these costs increase and decrease with the level of sales. Total variable costs as a percent of sales should remain relatively constant within the normal range of business activity in which your business typically operates.

Fixed costs are costs which happen whether a product or service is sold or not, such as rent, insurance, interest on debt, facilities, the salaries of office workers, advertising and promotion, and utility bills. Fixed costs in absolute terms (dollars rather than percentage) should also remain relatively constant within the normal range of business activity in which your business typically operates.

Your accountant can help you determine which costs are variable and which are fixed. It's worth the extra time and money to have this done, as you will soon see. If a cost seems to have elements of both variable and fixed costs, you could break it into its component variable and fixed costs. However, unless there is a real need for precision, this is generally more trouble than it's worth. Decide whether the item is primarily variable or fixed, and classify the whole item in that category.

When you subtract variable costs from sales you get a contribution margin, which is labeled as such because it is the portion of a sale that contributes to the payment of fixed costs and then to profit. Contribution margin is usually expressed as a percentage of sales or in dollars per unit, and is relatively constant within the normal range of business activity in which your business typically operates.

As an example, if you sell $1,000 worth of a product and your variable costs are $530, then the remaining $470 is your contribution margin. In this case, your variable cost is 53% of sales and your contribution margin is 47% of sales. If your sales consisted of a single product that you sold for $10.00, then your variable cost per unit would be 53% of $10.00, or $5.30. Your contribution margin per unit would be 47% of $10.00, or $4.70.

The key concept in breakeven analysis is that you start every month in a hole for the amount of your monthly fixed costs. You then apply the contribution margin from sales during the month against the fixed costs to fill that hole until you sell enough to breakeven. Once you breakeven, the contribution margin on additional sales is applied to profit.

As an example, let's assume that you have fixed costs of $40,000 per month. In breakeven analysis, conceptually you start each month with a $40,000 loss. You have to sell products with a positive contribution margin to make up that loss and then to make a profit. Let's also assume that the 47% contribution margin from the above previous example is your business's contribution margin and your monthly fixed costs are $40,000. How much do you have to sell to breakeven? The answer is $85,106 in sales with a 47% contribution margin will equal the $40,000 you incur in monthly fixed expenses.

The way to calculate your breakeven is to divide your fixed costs by your contribution margin percent. In this case

$40,000 Fixed Costs / 47% Contribution Margin equals $85,106 in Sales to break even
or
$40,000 Fixed Costs / .47 Contribution Margin equals $85,106 in Sales to break even.

To confirm multiply

$85,106 in Sales * 47% Contribution Margin equals your Fixed Costs of $40,000
or
$85,106 in Sales * .47 Contribution Margin equals your Fixed Costs of $40,000.

To calculate the breakeven unit count, let's use the previous $10.00 price per unit. The way to calculate your breakeven unit count is to divide your fixed costs by your contribution margin percent by your unit price. In this case

$40,000 Fixed Costs / 47% Contribution Margin / $10 product price equals 8,511 unit sales to breakeven.

Income Statement Formats

What follows is a comparison of an income statement in the traditional format to income statements in the breakeven format with various levels of detail. As you can see, the sales, cost of goods sold and profit are identical, but the way the information is categorized and displayed is totally different. The breakeven format supports your ability to project your breakeven point as well as to project your profitability in a variety of different situations.

Traditional Income Statement

XYZ Company		
P&L Report for Month Ended May 31		
Gross Sales	89,106	
Sales Returns and Allowances	(4,000)	
Sales Revenue	85,106	
Cost of Goods Sold	38,000	44.7%
Gross Margin	47,106	55.3%
Operating Expenses		
Salaries, Wages and Commissions	17,000	20.0%
Benefits and Taxes	4,000	4.7%
Office Expense	1,000	1.2%
Rent, Utilities and Services	12,000	14.1%
Sales, Marketing and Advertising	6,000	7.1%
Depreciation	1,106	1.3%
Other Expenses	4,000	4.7%
Total Operating Expenses	45,106	53.0%
Operating Profit	2,000	2.4%
Interest expense	2,000	
Net Income / Profit	0	0.0%

Breakeven Formatted Income Statement

XYZ Company		
P&L Breakeven for Month Ended May 31		
Sales Revenue	85,106	
Variable Expenses		
Cost of goods sold	38,000	44.7%
Variable operating costs	7,106	8.3%
Total Variable Expenses	45,106	53.0%
Contribution Margin	40,000	47.0%
Fixed Expenses		
Fixed operating costs	38,000	44.7%
Interest expense	2,000	2.4%
Total Fixed Expenses	40,000	47.0%
Profit	0	0.0%

Profitability Thinking

Expanded Breakeven Formatted Income Statement Designed to Further Explain How the Breakeven Formatted Income Statement Works

XYZ Company		
Expanded P&L Breakeven for Month Ended May 31		
Gross Sales	**89,106**	
Sales Returns and Allowances	(4,000)	
Sales Revenue	**85,106**	
Variable Expenses		
Cost of Goods Sold	38,000	44.7%
Delivery of merchandise and materials	1,000	1.2%
Shipping of finished goods to customers	1,000	1.2%
Sales commissions and bonuses	5,106	6.0%
Total Variable Expenses	**45,106**	**53.0%**
Contribution Margin	**40,000**	**47.0%**
Fixed Expenses		
Salaries	11,894	14.0%
Benefits and Taxes	4,000	4.7%
Office Expense	1,000	1.2%
Rent, Utilities and Services	12,000	14.1%
Sales, Marketing and Advertising	6,000	7.1%
Depreciation	1,106	1.3%
Other Expenses	2,000	2.4%
Interest Expense	2,000	2.4%
Total Fixed Expenses	**40,000**	**47.0%**
Profit	**0**	**0.0%**

A Simpler Breakeven Formatted Income Statement Designed to Support Breakeven Calculation

XYZ Company		
P&L Breakeven for Month Ended May 31		
Sales Revenue	85,106	
Total Variable Expenses	45,106	53.0%
Contribution Margin	40,000	47.0%
Total Fixed Expenses	40,000	47.0%
Profit	0	

Once you get past breakeven, your contribution margin of 47% of sales is profit as the fixed costs have already been paid for. The breakeven calculation can then be used to project profits. To illustrate, what if your sales were $120,000? How much would your profit be then? The answer is

$120,000 Sales * 47% Contribution Margin equals $56,400. Your Fixed Costs are still $40,000 as they typically don't change during the month. So your Profit is $56,400 Contribution Margin minus the $40,000 in Fixed Costs equaling $16,400 in Profit.

One more example. What if you only sold $60,000? What would your profit/loss be then? The answer is

$60,000 Sales * 47% Contribution Margin equals $28,200. Your Fixed Costs are still $40,000. $28,200 Contribution Margin minus $40,000 Fixed Costs equals a Loss of $11,800.

Below are what the breakeven formatted income statements might look like for the two examples with sales of $120,000 and $60,000 described above.

Breakeven Income Formatted Statement for $120,000 Sales

XYZ Company		
P&L Breakeven for Month Ended May 31		
Sales Revenue	120,000	
Variable Expenses		
Cost of goods sold	53,580	44.7%
Variable operating costs	10,020	8.4%
Total Variable Expenses	63,600	53.0%
Contribution Margin	56,400	47.0%
Fixed Expenses		
Fixed operating costs	38,000	31.7%
Interest expense	2,000	1.7%
Total Fixed Expenses	40,000	33.3%
Profit	16,400	13.7%

Profitability Thinking

Breakeven Income Formatted Statement for $60,000 Sales

XYZ Company		
P&L Breakeven for Month Ended May 31		
Sales Revenue	**60,000**	
Variable Expenses		
Cost of goods sold	26,790	44.7%
Variable operating costs	5,010	8.4%
Total Variable Expenses	**31,800**	**53.0%**
Contribution Margin	**28,200**	**47.0%**
Fixed Expenses		
Fixed operating costs	38,000	63.3%
Interest expense	2,000	3.3%
Total Fixed Expenses	**40,000**	**66.7%**
Profit	**(11,800)**	**-19.7%**

**For a free breakeven calculator, please go to
www.profitabilitythinking.com.**

Can you see how using your company's financials in this way allows you to determine if what you are doing to manage your business is leading to an acceptable level of profitability? If you know your sales and you know your contribution margin and you know your fixed costs, you can project your profit. Breakeven analysis allows you to do "what if" analysis, changing any of the variables to project a profit level under those projected conditions. This is sometimes called cost/volume/profit analysis or profit modeling. For our purposes, we will use the term profit projection. Once you can do profit projection calculations, the next step is to devise strategies to influence those variables and create the projected level of profit in reality. That's Profitability Thinking.

One word of caution about using profit projection. This model assumes that the product mix is constant, changes in sales activity are the only things that affect total variable costs in a given range of sales activity and there are no effects from inventory valuation issues. As such, it's not an extremely precise tool. However, it is directionally correct, produces reasonably accurate results and will aid in decision making. I have used profit projection calculations many times to project the profitability of businesses decisions I have made in businesses I have managed and found them to be quite useful.

Breakeven Analysis for Service Businesses

Breakeven analysis for service businesses works much the same way that breakeven analysis works for businesses that sell products, except that the numbers look slightly different. As explained in the previous chapter, typically there is no cost of goods sold for a business that only sells services, so all the variable expenses are variable operating costs which may be much less as a percentage of sales than for a business that sells products. Conversely, a service business's fixed operating costs as a percentage of sales tends to be much higher.

Below is an example of a breakeven formatted income statement for a business that sells only services.

Breakeven Formatted Income Statement for a Service Business

XYZ Company		
P&L Breakeven for Month Ended May 31		
Sales Revenue	85,106	
Variable Expenses		
Cost of goods sold	-	0.0%
Variable operating costs	13,106	15.4%
Total Variable Expenses	13,106	15.4%
Contribution Margin	72,000	84.6%
Fixed Expenses		
Fixed operating costs	70,000	82.3%
Interest expense	2,000	2.4%
Total Fixed Expenses	72,000	84.6%
Profit	0	0.0%

The breakeven calculation for the service business is the same as for the product business: fixed costs / contribution margin percent. The implication from the above service business breakeven formatted income statement is that the service business starts each month in a much deeper hole than the product business example we used. You may recall that the example product business started each month in a $40,000 fixed cost hole, and a 47% contribution margin from sales was what filled the hole and then created profit. In the above service business example, the business started in a $72,000 fixed cost hole, but had an 86.4% contribution margin from sales to fill the fixed cost hole and then create profit.

This is called leverage. In the example, if the service business can get above breakeven, it will start being much more profitable than the business that sells products because 84.6% of its sales are going to profit rather than the 47% for the product business. The risk is that with a deeper fixed cost hole to fill, if the service business doesn't create enough sales to make the breakeven point, it will lose much more money than the product business in our example.

The concept of leverage has implications to the business that sells products as well. What if the product business could buy an asset that increased its fixed costs but decreased its variable costs? Then the product business starts to take on more of the risks and opportunities of the service business example above. It will have a deeper fixed cost hole to fill, but will also have a higher contribution margin percentage and thus the opportunity to make more profit if it can get above breakeven.

Test Your Knowledge

Like learning a new language, learning math or learning a new golf swing, the best way to know that you have mastered the skill is to practice. So below are three problems that will allow you to go through the steps of figuring a breakeven point and project a profit. They will only take a few minutes, but will increase the likelihood that you will retain what you've learned and also verify in your own mind that you can do these kinds of calculations. Once you know you can do these quick calculations, you can use them in your own business to be more effective at managing its profitability. You can get the answers by going to **www.profitabilitythinking.com**.

Problem 1 - A business has a contribution margin of 40% and monthly fixed costs of $52,000. What is the breakeven point of the business?

_____

Problem 2 - A business has monthly sales of $90,000 and variable costs of $54,000, with monthly fixed costs of $30,000. What is the breakeven of the company? What is the profit at $90,000 sales?

_____

_____

Problem 3 - A business has a contribution margin of 30%, monthly fixed costs of $30,000 and a product sales price of $5. What is the monthly breakeven point in units?

PROFITABILITY THINKING

> ➤ **Have your accountant or a very good bookkeeper create a breakeven formatted income statement for your business, as well as for major divisions and product lines within your business on a regular basis. Depending on the complexity of the information, this might be easily done yourself.**
> ➤ **Calculate your breakeven point and project a likely profitability level reflecting the goals of your current business initiatives using the information provided in this section.**
> ➤ **Knowing your breakeven point and having the ability to project profits under various scenarios will improve your ability to make basic decisions about your business and avoid costly mistakes because you will understand the likely effects of decisions before you make them.**
> ➤ **Make plans to improve your contribution margin by raising prices, reducing the cost of goods sold, reducing variable operating costs or changing the mix of products you sell to focus on the more profitable items.**
> ➤ **Create incentives with your sales people to change your product sales mix by selling more profitable items or up-selling additional profitable items.**

What are Your Business's Metrics?

Information has no value unless it's used, so here's one of the places I'm asking you to do some homework, find out some information about your business and use it. In this case, what are your current monthly sales, contribution margin percent and monthly fixed costs? Then I 'd like you to calculate the breakeven for your business as well as what your profitability should be using this model given your level of sales. If you have an accurate contribution margin percentage and fixed cost amount, your calculation should be relatively close to your actual profit results, although they won't be exact. This is the first step in managing your business more effectively. In the next chapter, we'll explore how to use these calculations.

My business's current monthly sales are: _____

My business's current contribution margin % is: _____

My business's current monthly fixed costs are: _____

My business's current breakeven point is: _____

_____

My business's current monthly profit is: _____

My business's calculated profit projection using breakeven analysis is:

_____

Is your calculated profit projection relatively close to your actual profit, once you factor out onetime events? It should be. If not, check your sales amount, fixed cost amount and contribution margin percentage. It's important that you get these numbers directionally correct, because if they're not, your calculations to support your management decisions using this tool will be off. And there are a lot of uses for this tool.

Contribution Margin Percentage and Fixed Costs are Stable to a Point

Now that you understand the concept of breakeven analysis and profit projection, there are some things you should know that can change the outcome of your breakeven analysis and profit projections. These are mainly a function of your capacity utilization.

When Fixed Costs and Contribution Margin Percent Change

As previously mentioned, contribution margin percentages and fixed costs don't generally change in the short run. However, they are predicated on a range of volumes similar to your recent operation and sales history. That is to say, they reflect the normal range of your recent capacity utilization. This holds true for service businesses as well as product businesses.

To illustrate, what if your current operating results were at breakeven, and your unit sales and hence your production increase dramatically? Now your production team will have to work overtime to fill your increased order volume at a labor rate of time and a half per hour. What if you run short of component parts for your finished products because of the unplanned increase in sales volume? Now you have to express ship the components to keep your plant running. Will these changes in your operation change your contribution margin percent? Yes.

Your cost of goods sold component of your variable costs was based on your production team's labor rate calculated at straight time. Now there is overtime paid at a higher labor rate, increasing your variable costs as a percent of sales. Also, part of the cost of the component parts you used to manufacture your product was the cost to ship them to you. Your parts were historically delivered by normal surface transportation at less cost than the express shipment used to bring in needed parts because you were running out. This also raised the variable costs as a percent of sales. With your labor costs inflated due to overtime and material costs inflated due to express shipping of your component parts, your cost of goods sold will be inflated, increasing your variable costs as a percent of sales and decreasing your contribution margin percent of sales.

This kind of thing happens all the time and should be taken into consideration when making business decisions regarding increasing or decreasing your sales volume levels. Now imagine that the reason for the increased sales volume was that you cut your price 10% to get more business, reducing your gross margin and your contribution margin. Now you have all these extra orders that are costing you more to produce as a percent of sales than you thought. With the reduced price and increased costs, where is your contribution margin now? What is your breakeven now? And by the way, in volume increase situations like this, your fixed costs are not always as fixed as you thought they were.

Your fixed costs used in your breakeven analysis assumed that your support staff was constant. However, due to increased call volume you bring in another customer service representative. This new person now needs a computer to do the job so you purchase one and buy the software licenses. You need more space to store your component parts and finished goods because of the added volume so you rent a small space across the street. All of this adds to your fixed costs. You have a lower contribution margin supporting a higher fixed cost increasing your breakeven point.

Let's see what this looks like using the example above. Now let's assume that instead of a contribution margin of 47%, due to variable cost increases caused by overtime and the express shipment of component parts, along with the price decrease described above, your contribution margin is now 30%. Also, instead of fixed costs being $40,000, due to the extra customer service rep, the new computer

Profitability Thinking

and the added storage space you need, your fixed costs are now $46,000. Your old breakeven was $85,106 in sales for the month. What is it now? The answer is

$46,000 Fixed Costs / 30% Contribution Margin equals $153,333 in Sales to breakeven.

That's an 80% sales dollar increase to your breakeven. Oops! Worse, the breakeven unit count increased by 100% of the previous break even unit count as you are selling each unit for 90% of your previous price in your efforts to increase sales.

To calculate the breakeven unit count use the following calculation:

$46,000 Fixed Costs / 30% Contribution Margin / $9.00 unit sales price ($10 per unit minus the 10% discount) equals 17,037 units to breakeven.

That's a 100% increase over the 8,511 previous breakeven units!

So my question is, is it worth it to create this level of risk to the business and still be at breakeven, which is where you started? If your operating results at the beginning of the scenario were above or below breakeven, the resulting outcomes would be similar in nature. Remember, you will also need an additional level of available working capital to support the added production as you will need to pay for the increased material and labor before you receive cash from the additional sales from your customers. Do you have, or have access to, the required additional working capital? More about working capital levels later in the book.

This example is not all that farfetched. The point of the story is to understand your current production capacity and the effects of operating outside of it before making sales, pricing and production decisions. By doing the work up front to understand what the likely result of your decisions will be, you can avoid some costly mistakes and their inherent crises, and focus on business activities that show the most promise. That really is Profitability Thinking.

Notes

_____

_____

_____

_____

_____

_____

_____

_____

_____

_____

_____

_____

_____

_____

_____

Notes

_____

_____

_____

_____

_____

_____

_____

_____

_____

_____

_____

_____

_____

_____

_____

Chapter 5
The Profit Impact of Pricing, Investment and Marketing Decisions
Pre-Chapter Summary

1. This chapter includes:
   - ➤ Using breakeven analysis and profit projection to manage pricing
   - ➤ Using breakeven analysis and profit projection to manage investment decisions
   - ➤ Investing in new capacity
   - ➤ Advertising and marketing planning
   - ➤ Using breakeven analysis and profit projection for marketing

2. Have a pricing strategy that is part of your overall marketing plan. Pricing should not be decided ad-hoc on a day to day basis. In order to create an optimal pricing strategy, do the math of breakeven analysis and profit projection to create the best combination of price and volume.

3. If you cut your prices, then your contribution margin decreases and your breakeven increases. So why not raise your prices? That would increase the contribution margin and lower the breakeven point. Raising prices and losing a few customers might be a way to increase profitability, especially if you are at the upper limits of capacity. Do profit projection calculations to find out.

4. Breakeven analysis and profit projection can be used to test the increase in sales and contribution margin necessary to justify an investment in your business. This can be a machine to manufacture more product or a new product, another truck to make service calls, or an extra person in customer service to manage additional incoming calls.

5. Having a marketing plan and measuring the results of its execution will help you manage the profitability of your marketing activities. Although there are a lot of things that go into a marketing plan, two of the things the plan should include are the goals for the advertising and marketing, and a budget.

6. The goals of your advertising and marketing plan should include what it's trying to accomplish in terms of brand awareness, brand positioning or sales increases. Before you develop any marketing collateral, material or activities, there should be well defined and measurable goals.

7. In order to project the effect of your advertising and marketing activities, you will also need a budget. This will define the cost part of the cost benefit equation. Once you have a budget, a desired outcome and some other metrics like conversion rates, you can start to calculate whether the likely benefit is worth the proposed cost.

8. PROFITABILITY THINKING

> ➤ Use breakeven analysis and profit projection to increase the profitability of your pricing decisions and to understand their effects to the bottom line.

> ➤ Raising prices might just be your quickest route to increase the profitability of your business and lowering prices may just be the quickest way to decrease profitability.

> ➤ Test your assumptions and see if there is an opportunity to improve profitability by manipulating pricing and volume assumptions. Are there ways to raise prices without affecting (or minimally affecting) your sales volume?

> ➤ Calculate the contribution margin on everything you sell. Are you happy with all the contribution margins for your products and services?

> ➤ Assess your business's capacity and compare it to current business levels, especially if you are paying overtime or absorbing unusual expenses to make up for the lack of capacity.

> ➤ Determine if adding capacity might be a better alternative by projecting the profitability of an investment in your business.

> ➤ Assess whether you are better off renting or buying equipment. This will largely hinge on your cash position and your estimate of the sustainability of added business.

> ➤ Create a marketing and advertising budget as part of an overall marketing plan determined in advance of any marketing spend.

> ➤ Use breakeven analysis and profit projection to quantify the required profit necessary to proceed with a marketing spend.

> ➤ Measure the results of every marketing spend you make. Did it create the level of added sales and profit necessary to justify the expense? If yes, repeat. If no, try something else. Unless you measure, you won't know whether your spend was profitable.

> ➤ Measure the return on investment of your marketing against alternatives. Just because a marketing spend was profitable doesn't necessarily mean that it was the most profitable of all the alternatives. Always try to increase your marketing return on investment by testing and improving marketing spends to create the maximum return on your marketing investment.

Chapter 5
The Profit Impact of Pricing, Investment and Marketing Decisions
Profitability Thinking in Action

Using Breakeven Analysis and Profit Projection to Manage Pricing

Pricing is one thing in business that you have to get right. Price too high and you may not have enough customers and sales to breakeven. Price too low and you may not have enough contribution margin to breakeven. So, on what basis do you price your products? Let's consider a few types of pricing strategies.

> ➤ Cost plus pricing is adding a margin to whatever your total costs are for producing the product, purchasing the merchandise or supplying the service. However this approach doesn't take into consideration what your customers are willing to pay - possibly higher or lower. If you use this pricing method, you should know the total cost of producing your product or service so as not to price below that level.

A brief note about total costs. Your total cost per unit will be your total costs (cost of goods sold plus your fixed costs) divided by the number of units produced. A unit can be anything from a widget to a service call. Since your units produced varies but your fixed costs may not, your fixed cost per unit will vary. Imagine $10,000 in fixed costs divided by 1,000 units produced will equal $10 per unit in fixed costs. Now imagine the same $10,000 in fixed costs divided by 8,000 units produced will equal $12.50 per unit in fixed costs. Assuming your direct cost per unit is the same either way ($0 for services and COGS per unit for products), your fully loaded cost per unit will vary by $2.50 in this example depending on the production quantity.

For this reason, I've never been a fan of making decisions based on fully loaded costs. However, it will put you in the ball park and extra information is always useful. Given the above, I recommend that you use breakeven analysis and profit projection as a tool to fix your pricing.

> ➤ Market penetration pricing that tries to gain a foothold in a market with low pricing, with the thought (hope) that you can raise prices later.
> ➤ First to market premium pricing where you have little competition in the beginning, so you charge more.

➢ Giving a product away or pricing at a loss when you plan to sell another product due to the sale of the first product. Think razors and razor blades, printers and ink cartridges, and cell phones and rate plans.

➢ Raising prices because demand is outstripping your capacity. Rather than erode contribution margins with extra costs associated with producing beyond normal capacity, you raise your prices to get maximum contribution margin at the high end of normal capacity. This is a good short term solution to unusually high demand, however if the demand is sustainable, you should do the math to see if there is an appropriate strategy to expand your normal production capacity. More about investing in capacity later in the book.

➢ Loss leader pricing where you sell a product at low or no profit to attract customers who will buy other products you sell that aren't related to the original product. This is a traffic building strategy often found in retail.

Your pricing strategy might be one of these or none of these. However, you should have a pricing strategy that is part of your overall marketing plan. Pricing should not be decided ad-hoc on a day to day basis. In order to create an optimal pricing strategy, do the math of breakeven analysis and profit projection to create the best combination of price and volume. As an aside, this is why what I call profit projection is sometimes called cost/volume/profit analysis.

In the previous section, I alluded to what happens if you cut your price as a way to increase business. Basically, if you cut your price, then your contribution margin decreases and your breakeven increases. So why not raise your prices? That would increase the contribution margin and lower the breakeven point. To which I hear you say, "If I could I would, but if I did I'd lose customers." No doubt market realities will influence your pricing. But can you quantify your estimation of market realities? Let's do an experiment.

Let's assume your business has sales of $100,000 per month, has a contribution margin of 47% and fixed costs of $40,000 per month. That would mean that your business is making

$100,000 * 47% = $47,000 - $40,000 = $7,000 per month in profits.

Also, let's assume that your price per unit is $10, so you're selling 10,000 units per month. Your variable costs are $5.30 per unit. You face three alternatives:

A. Keep the pricing the same with no change in volume
B. Decrease prices 10% and assume you'll sell 15% more units
C. Raise your prices by 10% and assume a 15% loss in unit sales

Which would you do? This is where doing the math before making a pricing decision can be very important. Let's go through the alternatives.

A. Alternative A is 10,000 units sold * $10 per unit = $100,000 in sales. 10,000 units * $5.30 per unit in variable costs = $53,000 in variable costs leaving a $47,000 contribution margin. $47,000 in contribution margin - $40,000 fixed costs = $7,000 in profit.
A quicker way to calculate this is

$$(\$10-\$5.30)*10,000=\$47,000-\$40,000=\$7,000.$$

XYZ Company		
P&L Breakeven for Month Ended May 31		
Sales Revenue	100,000	
Total Variable Expenses	53,000	53.0%
Contribution Margin	47,000	47.0%
Total Fixed Expenses	40,000	40.0%
Profit	7,000	7.0%

B. Alternative B is 11,500 units (15% increase) sold * $9 (10% discount) per unit = $103,500 in sales. 11,500 units * $5.30 per unit in variable costs = $60,950 in variable costs leaving a $42,550 contribution margin. Assuming you can keep your fixed costs constant at $40,000, then $42,550 in contribution margin - $40,000 in fixed costs = $2,550 in profit.

A quicker way to calculate this is

$$(\$9-\$5.30)*11,500=\$42,550-\$40,000=\$2,550.$$

Another way to calculate if you don't have product cost is

$$\$100,000*1.15*.9=\$103,500, \text{ then } \$53,000*1.15=\$60,950, \text{ then}$$
$$\$103,500-\$60,950-\$40,000=\$2,550.$$

XYZ Company		
P&L Breakeven for Month Ended May 31		
Sales Revenue	103,500	
Total Variable Expenses	60,950	58.9%
Contribution Margin	42,550	41.1%
Total Fixed Expenses	40,000	38.6%
Profit	2,550	2.5%

C. Alternative C is 8,500 units (15% decrease) sold * $11 (10% increase) per unit = $93,500 in sales. 8,500 units * $5.30 per unit in variable costs = $45,050 in variable costs leaving a $48,450 contribution margin. $48,450 in contribution margin - $40,000 in fixed costs = $8,450 in profit.

A quicker way to calculate this is

($11-$5.30)*8,500=$48,450-$40,000=$8,450.

Another way to calculate if you don't have product cost is

$100,000*.85*1.1=$93,500, then $53,000*.85=$45,050, then $93,500-$45,050-$40,000=$8,450.

XYZ Company		
P&L Breakeven for Month Ended May 31		
Sales Revenue	93,500	
Total Variable Expenses	45,050	48.2%
Contribution Margin	48,450	51.8%
Total Fixed Expenses	40,000	42.8%
Profit	8,450	9.0%

As you can see from this set of alternatives, raising the price 10% and losing 15% of your unit sales volume is the most profitable short term alternative. This would be especially true if your fixed costs increased a little with increased unit sales and could be reduced a little with the unit sales decrease. That would accentuate the changes in profitability even further.

Now there are other considerations such as how will the loss of these sales and customers affect other product lines you might have or your ability to gain new business. These kinds of questions would need to answered in any pricing scenario. My point is to show you that raising prices rather than trying to increase volume by lowering prices is often the fastest way to increase profitability, if you can find a way to do it. In any event, doing the math will allow you to estimate the profitability of multiple alternatives and increase the likelihood your decision will increase profitability.

Test Your Knowledge

In this exercise, you're going to have the opportunity to evaluate three pricing alternatives. You will decide which alternative would be the best for the hypothetical business in the problem. The exercise is very similar to the pricing scenarios described in the previous section. For the correct answer, please go to **www.profitabilitythinking.com.**

Problem - You own a business with $50,000 per month in sales with $15,000 per month is fixed costs. You sell your product for $5 and have a contribution margin of 45%. As in the previous section's example, you have three strategy choices; to keep the price and volume the same, increase prices and lose volume, or decrease prices and gain volume. This is how you view your choices:

    A. Keep pricing and volume the same
    B. Increase prices 5% which you believe will decrease unit volume by 5%
    C. Decrease prices 5% which you believe will increase unit volume 5%

Given these choices, which strategy should be more profitable?

_____

_____

Are there reasons why you might go with an alternative that is not the most "profitable?" This is not a trick question and there is no correct answer. I just want you to give it some thought. There are a variety of consequences to any business decision, some of which don't immediately show up in the numbers. Taking a look at a business decision from many angles will increase the likelihood of making a good decision.

PROFITABILITY THINKING

➤ Use breakeven analysis and profit projection to increase the profitability of your pricing decisions and to understand their effects to the bottom line.

➤ Raising prices might just be your quickest route to increase the profitability of your business and decreasing prices may just be the quickest way to decreased profitability.

➤ Test your assumptions and see if there is an opportunity to improve profitability by manipulating pricing and volume assumptions. Are there ways to raise prices without affecting (or minimally affecting) your sales volume?

➤ Calculate the contribution margin on everything you sell. Are you happy with all of your products' contribution margins?

What are Your Business's Metrics?

Examine the pricing and volume of a product in your own business or of your business as a whole. Create three alternative scenarios, one of which is your current pricing and volume. What are the implications to your business' profitability?

Product - _____

Scenario 1 - _____

Scenario 2 - _____

Scenario 3 - _____

Conclusion from Scenarios - _____

Using Breakeven Analysis and Profit Projection to Manage Investment Decisions

Plant, equipment and personnel are your investment in the capacity of your business to go to market with a product or a service, and as such, your potential to produce profit. Obviously, having adequate capacity that supports your sales level without any extra expense for unneeded capacity is desirable. However, from time to time you may need to change your business's capacity to adjust for changes in demand - increased or decreased. In this section we are going to cover investment in expanded capacity to support additional sales.

Breakeven analysis and profit projection can be used to test the increase in sales and contribution margin necessary to justify an investment in your business. This can be a machine to manufacture more product or a new product, an extra person in customer service to manage additional incoming calls, or the addition of a truck to make more service calls.

You now know how to calculate your breakeven and how to project profits given a set of assumptions about your business. Using breakeven analysis and profit projection to manage investment decisions is just a slight modification of what you already know. If you don't feel comfortable with breakeven analysis and profit projection calculations, please go back over what we covered previously in this chapter and the previous chapter, and then come back when you are ready. Having the ability to do these quick calculations can save you from making mistakes and possibly save a great deal of money.

Investing in New Capacity

To show how you might use breakeven analysis and profit projection to screen for the profitability of a proposed investment in your business, consider the following situation. We'll use the business in the previous section that had sales of $100,000 per month, had a contribution margin of 47% and fixed costs of $40,000 per month. That would mean the business in the example is making $100,000 * 47% = $47,000 - $40,000 = $7,000 per month in profits. As in the previous example, let's assume that your price per unit is $10, so you're selling 10,000 units per month. Your variable costs are $5.30 per unit.

Suppose you now have the opportunity to lease a piece of equipment for $1,000 per month that will increase your contribution margin from 47% to 50%. You will also need one more employee at the cost of $3,500 per month in wages and benefits to operate the equipment.

For the sake of simplicity, we will assume that the additional expenses for both the equipment and the employee are fixed operating costs (I know that in a manufacturing setting the employee could be considered direct labor and be figured as part of cost of goods sold, but this would not be the case in a service business, so we'll simplify this example by making the employee a fixed cost).

So what in the business has changed? The first thing is that fixed costs per month have increased. How much? You have two additions to fixed costs to be calculated:

A. The $1,000 per month fixed costs for the equipment lease.
B. The $3,500 per month fixed costs for the employee.

So you have $1,000 per month lease cost plus $3,500 per month for the additional employee equals $4,500 in additional monthly fixed costs. Your old monthly fixed costs were $40,000, so your new monthly fixed costs are $44,500. Your contribution margin also changed from 47% to 50%. How much extra sales will be necessary to reach breakeven now, if any? The calculation is

$44,500 monthly Fixed Costs / 50% Contribution Margin = $89,000 in Sales to breakeven. Your old breakeven was $40,000 Fixed Costs / 47% Contribution Margin = $85,106.

You need $3,894 in additional monthly sales to reach the breakeven point of your new monthly expenses. Is it reasonable that your sales will increase $3,894 per month, or 390 units, to support the additional costs created by the equipment lease and the new employee? That's a management call. Having the correct numbers to make an informed decision is Profitability Thinking.

Now let's take a look at this in a different way. Assume the example we use is the one where the company is selling $100,000 worth of product with a 47% contribution margin and $40,000 in monthly fixed costs. You may recall the profit calculation for that company was $100,000 * 47% = $47,000 - $40,000 = $7,000 profit. So the question is, given the new fixed costs of $44,500 and new contribution margin of 50%, how much extra sales would be necessary to match the $7,000 per month in profitability? The calculation for this is

$44,500 new Fixed Costs + $7,000 which is the current Profit that you want to match = $51,500 / 50% Contribution Margin = $103,000 Sales for the month.

To confirm,

$103,000 * 50% = $51,500 - $44,500 = $7,000.

The old level of sales necessary to make $7,000 was $100,000. You need $3,000 more in monthly sales, or 300 more units, to match the previous level of profitability to justify the new equipment and new person.

Profitability Thinking

See below a breakeven formatted income statement for the current business condition in the example.

Breakeven Formatted Income Statement for Current Example of $100,000 Revenue

XYZ Company		
P&L Breakeven for Month Ended May 31		
Sales Revenue	100,000	
Total Variable Expenses	53,000	53.0%
Contribution Margin	47,000	47.0%
Total Fixed Expenses	40,000	40.0%
Profit	7,000	7.0%

Now see below the breakeven formatted income statement for the business after the addition of the new equipment and new employee with a better contribution margin.

Breakeven Formatted Income Statement for the Example With the New Equipment and New Employee

XYZ Company		
P&L Breakeven for Month Ended May 31		
Sales Revenue	103,000	
Total Variable Expenses	51,500	50.0%
Contribution Margin	51,500	50.0%
Total Fixed Expenses	44,500	43.2%
Profit	7,000	6.8%

Is an extra 300 units creating $3,000 in sales per month a reasonable expectation to produce and sell? It's your call, but a 3% increase in sales at the new contribution margin is typically not that significant an increase in production activity. So if you've got the business and it looks to be sustainable, you should consider adding the equipment and the person.

There is an additional consideration to all this and that is the decision to buy the equipment or to lease it. Although the lease option might be more expensive in the long run, there are two reasons you might consider leasing the equipment. They are that leasing reduces your business risk and requires less cash up front. If business declines, you can attempt to cancel the lease which might be easier and cheaper than trying to sell the used equipment. If cash is short, leasing might get you the added capacity without a large cash outlay.

Test Your Knowledge

In this exercise, your business is doing well. So well in fact, that you are consistently having to work your production team overtime and express ship orders to customers at your expense in order to meet delivery deadlines. It would really help if you had some extra production capacity to run your business without the overtime and be able to meet delivery deadlines without heroic measures.

Your business is currently selling $120,000 per month at a 45% contribution margin and $45,000 per month in fixed costs. You would like to lease a machine for $1,200 per month. You would also like to hire a person to run the machine at a cost for wages and benefits of $3,500 per month. Consider both of these additional expenses fixed operating costs. Please answer the two questions below. For the answers, please go to **www.profitabilitythinking.com**.

Problem 1 - What is your current monthly profit?

_____

Problem 2 - What would be the additional sales volume necessary to equal your current profitability after adding the machine and the employee?

_____

PROFITABILITY THINKING

> ➢ **Assess your business's capacity and compare it to current business levels, especially if you are paying overtime or absorbing unusual expenses to make up for the lack of capacity.**
> ➢ **Determine if adding capacity might be a better alternative by projecting the profitability of an investment in your business.**
> ➢ **Assess whether you are better off leasing or buying equipment. The decision will largely hinge on your cash position and your estimate of the sustainability of business levels.**

Profitability Thinking

Using Breakeven Analysis and Profit Projection to Manage Marketing Expenses

Do you advertise or engage in marketing activities that are intended to build your business's sales? How much do you spend? What additional sales have been generated by each of these advertising and marketing initiatives and expenses? Have you calculated the additional level of profitability, if any, that these sales and marketing initiatives, and expenses have generated?

I believe in spending money on sales and marketing, when I can see a clear return on my investment. For instance, say you were selling a big ticket item that had a contribution margin of $4,500 per unit (remember that the $4,500 is after commissions, which are variable costs). Your fully commissioned outside sales rep who will make a $2,500 commission on a sale of this product comes to you with a lead generation plan that would cost $100 per lead. You know that about one in ten of these leads results in a sale. The salesperson wants to split the $1,000 cost with you for lead generation activity that will produce ten leads. Would you take him up on his offer? There are a number of considerations to make this decision, but based solely on profitability, I would.

In the above example, the cost of the lead generation activity is split $500 to you and $500 to the salesperson, for a total of $1,000. With one sale likely to come from the 10 leads that cost $1,000, that is $1,000 lead cost per sale, or a $500 cost to you for the sale and a $500 cost to the salesperson for the sale. However, you get $4,500 in contribution margin for your $500 expense and the salesperson gets $2,500 in commission for his $500 expense. Unless there is a major downside to the sale, or activities leading to or fulfilling the sale, that sounds like a win all the way around.

In order to make this kind of a marketing decision, you would need a number of pieces of information such as:

> ➢ Your contribution margin for the sale of the item and your salesperson's commission for the sale of the item.
> ➢ The conversion rate of the leads generated and the cost per lead.

If you have this information, you can move forward with some confidence that this will be a winning business decision. If you don't have this information, you're flying blind and risk spending money on an unprofitable marketing activity or passing up a profitable marketing activity. Either one could cost you money.

I don't want to let this last statement pass without some emphasis. Obviously you don't want to make unprofitable marketing decisions. But passing up promising marketing decisions because of fear that you'll be wasting precious resources is also very expensive. As the great hockey player Wayne Gretzky is quoted as saying, "You miss 100% of the shots you don't take." If you are willing to do some math upfront, you will develop some confidence that the risk you're about to take with your resources will end up with a profitable outcome and you will be less likely to take a pass on promising marketing opportunities.

Advertising and Marketing Needs a Plan

Although we will cover business planning and budgeting later in this book, I wanted to spend a little time on this topic now. Using breakeven analysis and profit projection is a tool to aid in the decisions necessary to manage marketing expenses. Having a plan and measuring the results of the execution of the plan will help you manage the profitability of your marketing activities. Although there are a lot of things that go into a marketing plan, two of the things the plan should include are the goals for the advertising and marketing, and a budget.

The goals of your advertising and marketing plan should include what it's trying to accomplish in terms of brand awareness, brand positioning or sales increases. Before you develop any marketing collateral, material or activities, there should be well defined and measurable goals. Otherwise all you are doing is wishing and hoping.

As in the example of the salesperson's lead plan, there should be clear metrics as to what constitutes success. If you are trying to increase sales directly, then by how much? What is the cost of the extra sales and what is the extra contribution margin from those sales? What will be the return on the money invested?

In order to project the effect of your advertising, you will also need a budget. This will define the cost part of the cost benefit equation. Once you have a budget, a desired outcome and some other metrics like conversion rates, you can start to calculate whether the likely benefit is worth the proposed cost. You can also go back and see if the benefit you received is what you expected, and if your advertising and marketing efforts made money. Doing all of this is critically important in using your money in a way that benefits your business. In that respect, it's no different than the example of investing in new equipment in the last section of this chapter.

Using Breakeven Analysis and Profit Projection for Marketing

Suppose we take the company in the previous examples and use it to do the breakeven and profit projection calculations for an advertising spend. We will use the 47% contribution margin we previously used for that company. Now assume you want to spend $5,000 for advertising to increase sales. How much additional sales will be necessary to breakeven on the ad spend? The answer is

$5,000 ad spend / 47% contribution margin from additional sales = $10,638 in additional sales volume to breakeven on the ad spend. If the units are still $10, then that's an additional 1,064 units.

I realize nothing is ever that cut and dry. The customers attracted by the advertising might buy other things you sell or become repeat customers, buying more of the same item in the future. To the extent possible, try and estimate and quantify the residual value of these additional sales. That is part of the breakeven calculation. However, understand that these residual sales might be far into the future for a cost you are absorbing now. Can your business handle that kind of investment in possible benefits far into the future?

Now that we have done a simple breakeven on an ad spend, let's review an example calculating the benefit to a company of a successful ad spend. Suppose your business's sales are $90,000 per month with a contribution margin of 47%. Your fixed costs are $40,000 per month. Suppose you spend the above $5,000 on an ad spend to improve sales and the sales for the next three months are $300,000. That's $30,000 more than you might have expected with normal monthly sales of $90,000 per month ($90,000 * 3 = $270,000). You can't identify any other cause for the sales increase such as seasonality, so the sales increase must be as a result of the advertising. Let's go through the numbers.

The projected profit from your normal sales over the three month period is

$90,000 * 3 = $270,000 * 47% = $126,900 Contribution Margin for the 3 months.
$40,000 * 3 = $120,000 Fixed Costs for the 3 months.
$126,900 - $120,000 = $6,900 Profit for the 3 months.

The new profit is as follows.

$300,000 * 47% = $141,000 Contribution Margin for the 3 months with Fixed Costs still at $120,000.
$141,000 - $120,000 - $5,000 ad spend = $16,000
$16,000 new Profit - $6,900 old Profit = $9,100 additional Profit that can be inferred from the $5,000 ad spend.

A simpler way to calculate this is

$300,000 - $270,000 = $30,000 * 47% = $14,100 - $5,000 - $9,100.

That's an 82% return on the investment ($9,100 / $5,000 = 182% - 100% = 82%).

You will notice I said that the additional $9,100 additional profit can be inferred from the $5,000 ad spend. There is no way to know for sure whether the ad spend created the extra sales. Your best judgment says that it was. That's all you have to go on. But making informed judgments is what business management is all about. The purpose of this book is to give you the tools to make informed judgments. That's Profitability Thinking.

Assume your company spent $4,000 on an ad spend to increase sales. Sales improved $40,000 with a 47% contribution margin. Fixed costs stayed the same. For the correct answers to these problems, please go to **www.profitabilitythinking.com.**

Problem 1 - What is the additional sales volume necessary to breakeven on the ad spend?

———————————————————————————————

Problem 2 - What is the additional profit generated by the $4,000 ad spend that created the $40,000 in additional sales?

———————————————————————————————

PROFITABILITY THINKING

> ➤ **Create a marketing and advertising budget as part of an overall marketing plan determined in advance of any advertising or marketing spend.**
> ➤ **Use breakeven analysis and profit projection to quantify the required contribution margin necessary to proceed with a marketing spend.**
> ➤ **Measure the results of every marketing spend you make. Did it create the level of added sales and contribution margin necessary to justify the expense? If yes, repeat. If no, try something else. Unless you measure, you won't know whether your spend was profitable or not.**
> ➤ **Measure the return on investment of your marketing against alternatives. Just because a spend was profitable doesn't necessarily mean that it was the most profitable of all the alternatives. Always try to increase your marketing return on investment by testing and improving marketing spends to create the maximum return on your marketing investment.**

Summary

Breakeven analysis and profit projection are essential tools to help make profitable business decisions. They can help making pricing decisions, investment decisions and marketing decisions. If you do the calculations, I promise you that you will find a whole new way of looking at your business. One that makes understanding the numbers part of every business decision.

Remember that these tools work in a normal range of sales and production levels. As in the example, if you start changing how you do your business in order to accommodate large amounts of additional sales, these numbers won't hold up. To avoid unpleasant profitability surprises, be keenly aware of process changes driven by additional volume and start to make decisions about pricing and capacity as soon as possible based on new information.

Notes

_____

_____

_____

_____

_____

_____

_____

_____

_____

_____

_____

_____

_____

_____

_____

_____

Notes

Chapter 6
The Balance Sheet
Pre-Chapter Summary

1. This chapter includes:
- ➢ The contents of the Balance Sheet
- ➢ Spotting trends in the Balance Sheet

2. The balance sheet reports a business's financial position at a specific point in time as opposed to over a period of time, usually at the end of the month, the end of the quarter or the end of the year. The equations for the balance sheet are

Assets = Liabilities + Owner's Equity   or   Assets - Liabilities = Owner's Equity.

3. The contents of a balance sheet include:
- ➢ Assets
    - o Current Assets
    - o Fixed Assets
    - o Other Assets
- ➢ Total Assets
- ➢ Liabilities
    - o Current Liabilities
    - o Long-Term Liabilities
- ➢ Total Liabilities
- ➢ Owner's Equity
- ➢ Total Liabilities and Owner's Equity

4. If the balance sheet is detailed enough, it can be used to spot trends by comparing a series of balance sheets from consecutive time periods. Spotting trends is one way of using your business's metrics to manage your business better.

5. PROFITABILITY THINKING
- ➢ Make a commitment to read all of your financial statements including your balance sheet monthly with an eye toward finding improvement opportunities.

➢ Have your accountant or a very good bookkeeper create balance sheets for your business that show multiple units of time side by side. Make sure these balance sheets have enough line item detail to provide the information necessary to identify trends in specific areas of your business that can be managed. If you already have a series of individual balance sheets, it's fairly simple to put this information together yourself.
➢ Create profitability and cash flow improvement opportunities by spotting trends in your business.
➢ Develop plans to manage each area identified and take action.
➢ Based on your review of your financial statements, what was the trend in:
  o Cash?
  o Accounts Receivable?
  o Inventory?
  o Accounts Payable?
  o Current Assets?
  o Current Liabilities?
➢ What are your plans to address issues discovered?

6. What are your business's metrics? Please take the opportunity to review your business's metrics for the last three months in the following areas:

➢ Cash   _____   _____   _____

➢ Accounts Receivable   _____   _____   _____

➢ Inventory   _____   _____   _____

➢ Accounts Payable   _____   _____   _____

➢ Current Assets   _____   _____   _____

➢ Current Liabilities   _____   _____   _____

Chapter 6
The Balance Sheet
The Resources for Profitability Thinking

The Contents of the Balance Sheet

The balance sheet reports a company's financial position at a specific point in time as opposed to over a period of time, usually at the end of the month, the end of the quarter or the end of the year. It shows what the company's financial condition is at a point in time, but not how it got there. That happens with other financial reports and internal measuring tools. The balance sheet consists of assets which are what the company owns or is owed by others, liabilities which are what the company owes to others, and owner's equity which is what is left over after assets are subtracted from liabilities and represents the owner's investment in the business. Owner's equity is not what the company is worth or what it could be sold for. It's just what is left over, from an accounting point of view, when you subtract liabilities from assets. The equations for this are

Assets = Liabilities + Owner's Equity
or
Assets - Liabilities = Owner's Equity.

The Contents of the Balance Sheet

Assets are anything the company owns or is owed, and are generally divided into two categories which are current assets and fixed assets. Information in the asset portion of the balance sheet might include the following, and can include more.

Assets

- **Current Assets** - Cash and items that will be converted to cash or consumed within one year such as accounts receivable, inventory, prepaid expenses, notes receivable and other current assets.
  - **Cash and Equivalents** - Cash on hand, checking accounts, money market accounts and unrestricted bank accounts.
  - **Accounts Receivable** - Money owed from customers who purchased on credit. The product or service is delivered to your customer and you send an invoice. Those unpaid invoices are accounts receivable. Managing the amount and age of these receivables is critical to cash flow management.
  - **Inventory** - Raw materials, component parts, work in process and finished goods, as well as merchandise held for sale. Inventory is created when a company acquires an item that will ultimately be sold and is reduced as the items are sold. Inventory is acquired for cash (or accounts payable that will be paid out as cash), and may be sold for a receivable instead of cash. Converting items purchased as inventory, selling them and ultimately turning those sales into cash can take time. Cash will need to be invested to finance this process. Taking this time delay into consideration is also critical to cash flow management.
  - **Prepaid Expenses** - Items such as insurance which are paid for in advance for a specific period of time. The unused portion of that service has value and is a prepaid expense asset that will be consumed and expensed over time.
  - **Notes Receivable** - These are short-term loans made by the company, typically to customers, suppliers, employees or executives.
  - **Other Current Assets** - Assets that qualify to be current assets because they will be converted to cash or consumed within a year that don't neatly fit into the other categories.
- **Total Current Assets** - The total of all current assets listed above.
- **Fixed Assets** - Assets the company owns or is owed whose life exceeds one year such as land, buildings, machinery and equipment, capitalized leases, leasehold improvements, furniture and fixtures, deferred charges and other fixed assets.
  - **Land** - Land owned by the company.
  - **Buildings** - Buildings owned by the company.
  - **Machinery and Equipment** - Machinery and equipment whose cost is large enough to be capitalized and depreciated, and has value to the business that exceeds one year.
  - **Capitalized Leases** - Often a lease with an option to buy. It can also be the future benefits of a lease.
  - **Leasehold Improvements** - Improvements made to a property such as redoing the interior of an office space. This is considered an asset and can be capitalized and depreciated, and has value to the business that exceeds one year.
  - **Furniture and Fixtures** - Furniture and fixtures that have a value to the business of over one year and are expensive enough to qualify as an asset that can be depreciated.
  - **Deferred Costs** - Costs paid for an anticipated future benefit that is greater than one year. Examples might be an advertising campaign or origination costs involved in obtaining a long term loan.
  - **Other Fixed Assets** - Fixed assets that don't fit into any of the above categories.
- **Total Fixed Assets** - The total of all fixed assets listed above.
- **Other Assets and Intangibles** - Things like the value of R&D, market research and goodwill.
- **Total Assets** - The value of all assets owned or owed to the company.

Liabilities are anything the company owes to others, and are generally divided into two categories: current liabilities and long-term liabilities. Owner's equity is an accounting function to show what is left over after subtracting liabilities from assets and represent the owner's investment in the business. It is not the value of the company. Information in the liability and owner's equity portion of the balance sheet includes the following, and probably more.

Liabilities
- **Current Liabilities**
  - ○ **Accounts Payable - Obligations due to suppliers for inventory, goods and services purchased on credit similar to the credit you extend to your customers. Taking advantage of credit offered by your suppliers is part of a cash management strategy.**
  - ○ **Notes Payable - Promissory notes payable within one year.**
  - ○ **Income Taxes Payable - Tax obligations payable within one year.**
  - ○ **Wages Payable - Accrued unpaid salaries and wages owed to employees.**
  - ○ **Accrued Expenses - Primarily payroll taxes, and employee benefits accruals such as pension funds and interest payable.**
  - ○ **Current Portion of Long Term Debt - Portion of long term debt payable within one year.**
  - ○ **Other Current Liabilities - Current liabilities that don't fit into any of the above current liabilities categories.**
- **Total Current Liabilities - The total of the current liabilities above. These are all payments that will be due within one year.**
- **Long Term Liabilities - Liabilities not payable within a year such as non-current portion of long term debt, deferred income taxes, notes payable to officers and owners, and other long term liabilities.**
  - ○ **Non-Current Portion of Long Term Debt - Portions of long term debt not payable within one year.**
  - ○ **Deferred Income Taxes - Taxes payable in the future for various reasons.**
  - ○ **Notes Payable to Officers and Owners - Officers and owners lend money to their company to increase working capital rather than buying additional stock.**
  - ○ **Other Long Term Liabilities - Long term liabilities that don't fit into the above categories.**
- **Total long term liabilities - The total of all long term liabilities listed above.**
- **Owner's Equity - Total assets minus total liabilities and represent the owner's share of funding the business. Owners equity can be divided into preferred stock at par value, common stock at par value, additional paid in capital and retained earnings.**
- **Total Liabilities and Owner's Equity - Total liabilities and owners equity always equals total assets.**

An example of a balance sheet using the above categories might look like the one below.

XYZ Company	
Balance Sheet as of December 31	
Assets	
Current Assets	
Cash and Equivalents	75,000
Accounts Receivable	125,000
Inventory	150,000
Prepaid Expenses	20,000
Notes Receivable	5,000
Other Current Assets	25,000
Total Current Assets	**400,000**
Fixed Assets	
Land	100,000
Buildings	150,000
Machinery and Equipment	100,000
Capitalized Leases	50,000
Leasehold Improvements	25,000
Furniture and Fixtures	50,000
(Less Accumulated Depreciation)	(150,000)
Deferred Costs	20,000
Other Fixed Assets	20,000
Total Fixed Assets	**365,000**
Total Assets	**765,000**
Liabilities	
Current Liabilities	
Accounts Payable	100,000
Notes Payable	35,000
Current Income Taxes Payable	10,000
Wages Payable	15,000
Accrued Liabilities	10,000
Current Portion of Long-Term Debt	30,000
Other Short-Term Liabilities	20,000
Total Current Liabilities	**220,000**
Long-Term Liabilities	
Non-current Long Term Debt	300,000
Deferred Income Taxes	15,000
Notes Payable to Officers and Owners	10,000
Other Long-Term Liabilities	50,000
Total Long-Term Liabilities	**375,000**
Total Liabilities	**595,000**
Equity	
Preferred and Common Stock	120,000
Retained Earnings	50,000
Total Equity	**170,000**
Total Liabilities and Equity	**765,000**

Spotting Trends in the Balance Sheet

Just as with income statements in an earlier chapter, balance sheets can be used to spot trends over sequential periods of time. The way to do this is to lay them side by side on the same report as in the following balance sheet example. What trends can you spot? We will go over this information in more detail in the next section as part of looking at ratios and financial risk.

XYZ Company			
Balance Sheet as of December 31	Year 1	Year 2	Year 3
Assets			
Current Assets			
Cash and Equivalents	45,000	35,000	75,000
Accounts Receivable	100,000	150,000	125,000
Inventory	150,000	160,000	150,000
Prepaid Expenses	10,000	15,000	20,000
Notes Receivable	5,000	5,000	5,000
Other Current Assets	25,000	25,000	25,000
Total Current Assets	**335,000**	**390,000**	**400,000**
Fixed Assets			
Land	100,000	100,000	100,000
Buildings	100,000	100,000	150,000
Machinery and Equipment	80,000	90,000	100,000
Capitalized Leases	50,000	50,000	50,000
Leasehold Improvements	25,000	25,000	25,000
Furniture and Fixtures	35,000	35,000	50,000
(Less Accumulated Depreciation)	(70,000)	(110,000)	(150,000)
Deferred Costs	20,000	20,000	20,000
Other Fixed Assets	20,000	20,000	20,000
Total Fixed Assets	**360,000**	**330,000**	**365,000**
Total Assets	**695,000**	**720,000**	**765,000**
Liabilities			
Current Liabilities			
Accounts Payable	90,000	110,000	100,000
Notes Payable	35,000	35,000	35,000
Current Income Taxes Payable	10,000	10,000	10,000
Wages Payable	10,000	12,000	15,000
Accrued Liabilities	10,000	10,000	10,000
Current Portion of Long-Term Debt	20,000	25,000	30,000
Other Short-Term Liabilities	20,000	20,000	20,000
Total Current Liabilities	**195,000**	**222,000**	**220,000**
Long-Term Liabilities			
Non-current Long Term Debt	250,000	250,000	300,000
Deferred Income Taxes	12,000	12,000	15,000
Notes Payable to Officers and Owners	10,000	10,000	10,000
Other Long-Term Liabilities	50,000	50,000	50,000
Total Long-Term Liabilities	**322,000**	**322,000**	**375,000**
Total Liabilities	**517,000**	**544,000**	**595,000**
Equity			
Preferred and Common Stock	120,000	120,000	120,000
Retained Earnings	58,000	56,000	50,000
Total Equity	**178,000**	**176,000**	**170,000**
Total Liabilities and Equity	**695,000**	**720,000**	**765,000**

Profitability Thinking

PROFITABILITY THINKING

➢ **Make a commitment to read all of your financial statements including your balance sheet monthly with an eye toward finding improvement opportunities.**

➢ **Have your accountant or a very good bookkeeper create balance sheets for your business that show multiple units of time side by side. Make sure these balance sheets have enough line item detail to provide the information necessary to identify trends in specific areas of your business that can be managed. If you already have a series of individual balance sheets, it's fairly simple to put this information together yourself.**

➢ **Create profitability and cash flow improvement opportunities by spotting trends in your business.**

➢ **Develop plans to manage each area identified and take action.**

➢ **Based on a review of your balance sheets, what was the trend in:**
  o **Cash?**
  o **Accounts Receivable?**
  o **Inventory?**
  o **Accounts Payable?**
  o **Current Assets?**
  o **Current Liabilities?**

➢ **What are your plans to address issues discovered?**

What are Your Business's Metrics?

To support the Profitability Thinking bullets above, please take the opportunity to review your business's metrics for the last three months in the following areas:

➢ **Cash**   _____   _____   _____

➢ **Accounts Receivable**   _____   _____   _____

➢ **Inventory**   _____   _____   _____

➢ **Accounts Payable**   _____   _____   _____

➢ **Current Assets**   _____   _____   _____

➢ **Current Liabilities**   _____   _____   _____

Notes

_____

_____

_____

_____

_____

_____

_____

_____

_____

_____

_____

_____

_____

_____

_____

_____

Chapter 7
Ratios that Measure Risk, Efficiency and Profitability
Pre-Chapter Summary

1. This chapter includes:
  ➤ Using ratios to determine the financial health and risk of your business
  ➤ Liquidity ratios
  ➤ Solvency ratios
  ➤ Efficiency ratios
  ➤ Profitability ratios

2. Balance sheet comparison ratios and percentages can be used as an indication of your business's:
  ➤ Liquidity
  ➤ Solvency
  ➤ Efficiency
  ➤ Profitability

3. Banks and suppliers routinely use business ratios to determine whether to extend credit to your business because they indicate its ability to meet financial obligations. You can use these ratios in the same way by becoming familiar with them to assess your business's own financial situation and to see your business the way banks and creditors see it.

4. Liquidity ratios show your business's ability to raise cash to cover obligations. The two liquidity ratios covered in the chapter are:
  ➤ The Current Ratio calculated as
    Current Assets / Current Liabilities = Current Ratio.
  ➤ The Quick or Acid Test Ratio calculated as
    Current Assets - (inventory + prepaid expenses) / Current Liabilities = Quick Ratio.

5. Solvency ratios are a measure of your business's ability to pay debt obligations regardless of cash flow. The two solvency ratios covered in the chapter are:
  ➤ The Debt to Equity Ratio calculated as
    Total Debt / Owner's Equity = Debt to Equity Ratio.
  ➤ The Debt to Assets Ratio calculated as
    Total Debt / Total Assets = Debt to Asset Ratio.

6. Efficiency ratios measure your business's ability to manage its resources and cash flow. The four efficiency ratios covered in the chapter are:

> ➤ The Accounts Receivable to Sales Ratio is calculated as
>> **Accounts Receivable / Monthly Sales = Accounts Receivable to Sales Ratio.**
> ➤ The Average Collection Period is calculated as
>> **Current Accounts Receivable Balance / (Annual Sales / 360) = Average Collection Period.**
> ➤ Inventory to Sales Ratio is calculated as
>> **Inventory / Monthly Sales = Inventory to Sales Ratio.**
> ➤ The Average Days of Inventory on Hand is calculated as
>> **Current Inventory / (Annual Cost of Goods Sold / 360) = Average Days Inventory on Hand.**

7. Profitability ratios are a measure of the return on the resources committed to your business. The two profitability ratios covered in this chapter that weren't covered in the income statement chapter are:

> ➤ Return on Assets calculated as
>> **Net Income / Total Assets = Return on Assets.**
> ➤ Return on Equity (also known as ROI) calculated as
>> **Net Income / Owners Equity = ROI.**

8. PROFITABILITY THINKING

> ➤ Calculate the liquidity, solvency, efficiency and profitability ratios for your business for each of the last three months.
> ➤ Is there a trend in either of the liquidity ratios you calculated that creates a concern in your mind regarding future cash availability?
> ➤ Are the amounts you have invested in accounts receivable and inventory heading in the right direction?
> ➤ Is your accounts payable greater than your accounts receivable? Are there steps you can take to create that situation without hurting your relationships with your customers or suppliers?
> ➤ Create a plan to manage each of these ratios and bring the problematic ones back into line.

Chapter 7
Ratios that Measure Risk, Efficiency and Profitability
Evaluating Profitability Thinking

Using Ratios to Determine the Financial Health and Risk of Your Business

As with the income statement in a previous chapter, the numbers in the balance sheet do not stand alone. They are in the context of other numbers - total current assets to current liabilities as an example. Balance sheet comparison ratios and percentages can be used as an indication of your business's:

- Liquidity
- Solvency
- Efficiency
- Profitability

Banks and suppliers routinely use business ratios to determine whether to extend credit to your business because they indicate its ability to meet financial obligations (to pay its bills). You can use these ratios in the same way by becoming familiar with them to assess your business's own financial situation and to see your business the way banks and creditors see it.

There are two ways ratios are expressed. If a business ratio is greater than 1:1, then it is expressed as a ratio such as 1:1, 2:1, 3:1, etc. If the ratio is less than 1:1, then it is expressed as a percentage, so .25 would become 25%.

For reference, I'm putting the balance sheet from the last chapter below.

XYZ Company	
Balance Sheet as of December 31	
Assets	
Current Assets	
Cash and Equivalents	75,000
Accounts Receivable	125,000
Inventory	150,000
Prepaid Expenses	20,000
Notes Receivable	5,000
Other Current Assets	25,000
Total Current Assets	**400,000**
Fixed Assets	
Land	100,000
Buildings	150,000
Machinery and Equipment	100,000
Capitalized Leases	50,000
Leasehold Improvements	25,000
Furniture and Fixtures	50,000
(Less Accumulated Depreciation)	(150,000)
Deferred Costs	20,000
Other Fixed Assets	20,000
Total Fixed Assets	**365,000**
Total Assets	**765,000**
Liabilities	
Current Liabilities	
Accounts Payable	100,000
Notes Payable	35,000
Current Income Taxes Payable	10,000
Wages Payable	15,000
Accrued Liabilities	10,000
Current Portion of Long-Term Debt	30,000
Other Short-Term Liabilities	20,000
Total Current Liabilities	**220,000**
Long-Term Liabilities	
Non-current Long Term Debt	300,000
Deferred Income Taxes	15,000
Notes Payable to Officers and Owners	10,000
Other Long-Term Liabilities	50,000
Total Long-Term Liabilities	**375,000**
Total Liabilities	**595,000**
Equity	
Preferred and Common Stock	120,000
Retained Earnings	50,000
Total Equity	**170,000**
Total Liabilities and Equity	**765,000**

Liquidity Ratios

Liquidity ratios generally indicate your business's ability to quickly raise cash to pay its bills. They are important as a problem revealed by one of these ratios could mean your business is at risk of not being able to pay its short-term financial obligations. For this reason, creditors and bankers often show particular interest in these ratios.

The two liquidity ratios covered in this chapter are:

> ➢ The Current Ratio
> ➢ The Quick or Acid Test Ratio

For a free tool to calculate your current ratio and quick ratio, go to www.profitabilitythinking.com.

Current Ratio - Probably the most commonly used ratio of any of the balance sheet ratios is the current ratio. It is the ratio of current assets to current liabilities and indicates your business's ability to generate enough cash to pay its short term obligations. The formula is

Current Assets / Current Liabilities = Current Ratio.

In the balance sheet example, the ratio is

$400,000 Current Assets / $220,000 Current Liabilities = 1.82:1 Current Ratio.

Although the number can vary by industry and situation, a good rule of thumb is a current ratio of 2:1 or better, that is your business's current assets are at least twice its current liabilities. If you start to see a decrease in this ratio, it could either be a decrease in current assets, or an increase in short-term debt and payables. In any event, a decrease indicates a reduced ability to generate cash sufficient to pay current obligations.

If you need to improve your current ratio, you will need to increase current assets or decrease current liabilities. This can be done by doing things like booking pending orders sooner (if this is possible) to increase accounts receivable, or postponing a purchase or investment to avoid increasing accounts payable. Also, as long as the current ratio is greater than 1:1, paying down current liabilities with current assets (cash) will reduce both by an equal amount, but improve the ratio between the two.

Quick or Acid Test Ratio - This ratio is similar in purpose to the current ratio. However, one of the problems with the current ratio is that it includes all current assets as an indication of your business's ability to pay current obligations.

This includes inventory and pre-paid expenses. However, inventory has to be sold to be turned into cash, which may or may not be possible to do quickly. Pre-paid expenses can't be turned into cash at all. Cash has already been paid for them and the value of the prepaid expense is the future benefits purchased, such as ongoing insurance coverage. The quick ratio (or acid test ratio) eliminates these current assets to more accurately assess your business's ability to generate cash to pay current obligations. The resulting revision of current assets is called quick current assets. The formula for the quick ratio is

Current Assets - (inventory + prepaid expenses) / Current Liabilities = Quick Ratio.

In the balance sheet example, the ratio is

$230,000 Quick Current Assets ($400,000 current assets - $150,000 inventory - $20,000 prepaid expenses) / $220,000 Current Liabilities = 1.05:1 Quick Ratio.

Again, the number can vary by industry or situation, but a good rule of thumb is a quick ratio of 1:1 or better, that is quick current assets are at least as much as current liabilities. As with the current ratio, this number can be improved by increasing quick current assets or decreasing current liabilities. Increasing quick current assets can be done by doing things like booking pending orders sooner (if this is possible) to increase accounts receivable or converting inventory to cash. Decreasing current liabilities can be done by minimizing accounts payable which can be accomplished by postponing a purchase or investment.

Solvency Ratios

Solvency ratios are another set of ratios that measure your business's financial risk. In this case, your ability to pay debt obligations regardless of cash flow. Generally this means the less debt the better.

The two solvency ratios covered in this chapter are:

➢ Debt to Equity
➢ Debt to Assets

Debt to Equity - The debt to equity ratio measures your business's leverage employed to increase profits. With this ratio, total debt is compared with owner's equity to create a ratio. The formula is

Total Debt / Owner's Equity = Debt to Equity Ratio.

Too large a debt burden may increase leverage and improve profitability, but too much debt may become too much for your business to manage and lead to

Profitability Thinking

bankruptcy. The lower this ratio, the less financial risk to your company. To improve this ratio you will need to reduce your debt by paying it off or increase your owner's equity by increasing retained earnings. Increasing retained earnings can be accomplished by postponing a purchase, investment or bonus payout.

Debt to Assets - This ratio shows how much of your business is financed by creditors. The formula for this is

Total Debt / Total Assets = Debt to Asset Ratio expressed as a percent.

As an example, suppose your business had $365,000 of debt and $765,000 of total assets. Then the calculation is

$365,000 / $765,000 = 47.7%.

As with other ratios, the number may vary by industry and situation, but a good rule of thumb is to have a debt to assets ratio of below 50%. Higher than that may indicate you have too much debt creating the possible risk that you won't be able to pay it. Paying off debt will improve this ratio.

Efficiency Ratios

Your business has finite resources. You will need to use them efficiently to manage cash flow and control costs. Your ability to use resources efficiently also has an effect on the cost competitiveness of your business. The ratios below will help you manage resources efficiently.

The four efficiency ratios covered in this chapter are:

> ➤ Accounts Receivable to Sales Ratio
> ➤ Average Collection Period
> ➤ Inventory to Sales Ratio
> ➤ Average Days of Inventory on Hand

After explaining these ratios in this chapter, we will visit them again in the chapter about cash flow management later in this book.

For a free tool to calculate your A/R to sales, average collection period, inventory to sales and average days inventory, please go to www.profitabilitythinking.com.

Accounts Receivable to Sales Ratio - Accounts receivable is uncollected money from sales made on credit to your customers. If your business extends credit to customers, most of the cash to run your business will come from the collection of accounts receivable. The accounts receivable to sales ratio looks at the ratio of uncollected receivables in comparison to your sales. Keeping track of this ratio will help identify problems with cash inflows. Problems with cash inflows could indicate future cash flow problems for your business.

The way to calculate this ratio is

Accounts Receivable / Monthly Sales = Accounts Receivable to Sales Ratio.

Keeping track of this ratio over time is a quick and easy way to manage your investment in accounts receivable. If your accounts receivable is growing faster than your monthly sales, then this might be the first sign of future cash flow problems.

As an example, if your current accounts receivable at the end of the month is $125,000 and your monthly sales are $100,000, then your accounts receivable to sales ratio would be 1.25:1. If the following month your accounts receivable is $135,000 and your sales are $90,000, then your accounts receivable to sales ratio would have increased to 1.5:1. This increase could be an early sign of cash flow issues developing. By calculating this ratio monthly and comparing the results over time, you will be able to see any unfavorable changes, and take action to increase collections or modify your credit policy to correct the situation before it causes problems for your business. Remember, the more you have invested in accounts receivable, the less cash you have available to operate your business.

Average Collection Period - This ratio, also known as the Days of Sales Outstanding, measures the length of time it takes to turn sales into cash. In other words, the average number of days to collect from your customers. The amount in your accounts receivable can be converted to the number of days of sales waiting to be collected. The longer the time, the longer it takes you to turn a sale into cash and the more you have invested in accounts receivable. As with the previous ratio, the more money you have invested in accounts receivable, the less cash you have to invest in your business or to pay bills.

The way to calculate the average collection period is

Current Accounts Receivable Balance / Average Daily Sales = Average Collection Period.

The formula to calculate the average daily sales component in the previous formula for average collection period is

Annual Sales / 360 = Average Daily Sales.

Profitability Thinking

A quicker way to state this formula is

Current Accounts Receivable Balance / (Annual Sales / 360) = Average Collection Period
or
(Current Accounts Receivable / Annual Sales) * 360 = Average Collection Period.

All of these formulas create the same result. Use the one that you're most comfortable with.

If your sales are changing dramatically, you might consider doing a quarterly average daily sales. This can be calculated as

Quarterly Sales / 90 = Average Daily Sales.

As an example of the average collection period, if your current accounts receivable balance is $125,000 and your sales for the year are $1,200,000, your average collection period would be

Average Daily Sales = $1,200,000 / 360 = $3,333 per day.

Average Collection Period = $125,000 / $3,333 = 37.5 days is the average period of time to collect from your customers and turn a sale into cash.

Inventory to Sales Ratio - Your inventory supports your sales and as such, should have a fairly constant relationship to one another. The formula to calculate this ratio is

Inventory / Monthly Sales = Inventory to Sales Ratio.

If sales increase, then inventory should increase by a similar percentage. For instance, if your inventory is $100,000 and your monthly sales volume is $80,000, then your inventory to sales ratio would be $100,000:$80,000, or 1.25:1. If your sales increased to $100,000, then it might very well be appropriate for your inventory to increase to $125,000, maintaining that 1.25:1 relationship. The increase in inventory to support the added sales may be an issue from a cash flow perspective as you would need to pay for it, but from an operational perspective it doesn't seem unreasonable, assuming the inventory was in line in the first place.

More on working capital requirements in the chapter about managing cash flow later in the book.

However, suppose your sales stayed the same at $80,000 but your inventory increased to $160,000. Now your inventory to sales ratio is 2:1. This may indicate a problem with your internal processes as well as a future cash flow issue, as you are increasing the cash invested in your business without adding sales that will lead to increased cash flow. Similarly, if your inventory stayed at $100,000 but your sales decreased to $50,000, your ratio would be 2:1 indicating the same issues.

Tracking over time the relationship of inventory to sales in the form of this ratio is a very quick and easy way to manage both your investment in inventory and cash flow.

Average Days of Inventory on Hand - Your business has inventory to support sales. As such, your inventory investment will support your sales for a period of time and then run out. Accordingly, the dollars you have invested in inventory can be converted to days of inventory on hand before it is sold. The longer the days of inventory on hand, the greater the investment in inventory required and the greater the pressure on cash flow. The obvious moral to this story is to only keep on hand what is required to support adequate fulfillment of sales orders and no more.

The way you measure average days of inventory on hand is

Current Inventory / Average Daily Cost of Goods Sold = Average Days Inventory on Hand.

The formula to calculate the average daily cost of goods sold component in the previous formula for average days of inventory on hand is

Annual Cost of Goods Sold / 360 = Average Daily Cost of Goods Sold.

If your sales are changing dramatically, you might consider doing a quarterly average daily cost of goods sold. This can be calculated as

Quarterly Cost of Goods Sold / 90 = Average Daily Cost of Goods Sold.

Let's use an example to make this concept clearer. If your current inventory is $150,000 and your cost of goods sold for the year is $636,000, your average days inventory on hand would be

Average Daily Cost of Goods Sold = $636,000 / 360 = $1,767 per day

Average Days Inventory on Hand = $150,000 / $1,767 = 84.9 Average Days of Inventory on Hand.

A quicker way to state this formula is

Current Inventory / (Annual Cost of Goods Sold / 360) = Average Days Inventory on Hand
or
(Current Inventory / Annual Cost of Goods Sold) * 360 = Average Days Inventory on Hand.

Again, this ratio varies by industry and situation. However, 85 days of inventory is unusually high for most businesses. In a situation like this, find out what items have the highest days on hand and manage those inventories down. Also, take a look at your top 20% sellers. Are there any of those products that can be managed down. Find out why these items got out of balance and correct that process. Finally, check your assumptions regarding future sales and lead times. Fixing an overstocked inventory can free up cash to use in other parts of the business.

Days Payable Outstanding - Similar to the average collection period, this ratio measures how many days sales are in your accounts payable. In other words, the average number of days of sales to pay your bills. The longer the time, the more payments pending in accounts payable. If your sales volume is stable and not declining, this situation can be a good thing as you have retained cash for a longer period of time.

The way to calculate days payable outstanding is

Current Accounts Payable Balance / Average Daily Sales = Days Payable Outstanding.

The formula to calculate the average daily sales component in the previous formula for average days payable outstanding is

Annual Sales / 360 = Average Daily Sales.

A quicker way to state this formula is

Current Accounts Payable Balance / (Annual Sales / 360) = Days Payable Outstanding
or
(Current Accounts Payable / Annual Sales) * 360 = Days Payable Outstanding.

All of these formulas create the same result.

If your sales are changing dramatically, you might consider doing a quarterly average daily sales. This can be calculated as

Quarterly Sales / 90 = Average Daily Sales.

As an example, if your current accounts payable is $100,000 and your sales for the year were $1,200,000, your days payable outstanding would be

Average Daily Sales = $1,200,000 / 360 = $3,333 per day

Days Payable Outstanding = $100,000 / $3,333 = 30.0 days is the average days of sales required to pay your bills.

The Float

Are your customers and suppliers financing your ongoing business operations? One way to think about this question is with the relationship of your accounts payable to your accounts receivable. If your accounts payable is greater than your accounts receivable, then you owe your suppliers a greater amount than you are owed by your customers. If your sales are stable and not declining, this typically means you are collecting from your customers faster than you are paying your suppliers, which means cash is flowing into your business.

Conversely if your accounts receivable is greater than your accounts payable, then you would be carrying your customers to a greater extent than your suppliers are carrying you. Cash is flowing out of your business. You have a cash flow gap.

As a general rule, although this may not always be possible, you should try and keep your accounts receivable less than your accounts payable. To the extent that you can do this, you are using a form of float. There are two ways to create a float:

> ➤ Collect from your customers faster
> ➤ Pay your bills slower

Any attempts to do this should be done without hurting your relationships with your suppliers or customers. We will cover strategies to do this in the chapter about cash flow management.

Profitability Ratios

You may recall from the previous chapter about income statements that there were two profitability ratios that used balance sheet information as well as income statement information. They are both measures of how well your business has done with the resources committed to its operation.

For a free tool to calculate your return on equity and return on assets, please go to www.profitabilitythinking.com.

Return on Assets - This ratio, also known as ROA, measures how effectively your business is using its assets to produce income. Although not a measure that can be managed directly, it does measure the relative performance of the assets employed and as such, will tell a story over time. The calculation for return on assets is

Net Income / Total Assets = Return on Assets expressed as a percent.

As an example, suppose your business had net income of $84,000 in the previous year and had $765,000 in total assets. The calculation would be

$84,000 / $765,000 = 11%.

Good ROA ratios vary by industry and situation. Industries with large asset requirements such as manufacturing and transportation might target 5% while software and service businesses might target 20% or more.

Return on Equity - Sometimes called return on investment or ROI, the return on equity ratio measures the return in the form of profits generated by your investment in the business. As such, your business's ROI should exceed what you could have earned in a substitute investment such as stocks, bonds, CDs or income producing real estate. This ratio measures how effectively you have invested your money.
The calculation for ROI is

Net Income / Owners Equity = ROI.

As an example, Suppose your business made $84,000 and your owner's equity was $170,000. That would calculate as

$84,000 / $170,000 = 49.4%.

As a general rule of thumb, a good ROI is more than 20%. The above example of 49.4% is very healthy given the alternatives of perhaps 3%-6% in bonds or high yielding stocks.

Test Your Knowledge

Assume your business has the following in its balance sheet:

- ➢ $50,000 in cash
- ➢ $50,000 in accounts receivable
- ➢ $200,000 in total current assets
- ➢ $110,000 in total current liabilities

What is the current ratio? _____

What is the current quick/acid test ratio? _____

As a rule of thumb, should you happy with the results of your calculations? Why?

_____

Assume your business has the following in its income statement and balance sheet:

- ➢ $500,000 in sales
- ➢ 55% cost of goods sold
- ➢ $50,000 in accounts receivable
- ➢ $40,000 in accounts payable
- ➢ $80,000 in inventory

What is the average daily sales? _____

What is the average daily cost of goods sold? _____

What is the average collection period? _____

What is the average days of inventory on hand? _____

In your opinion, are any of these ratios problematic? Why?

_____

For the answers to these question, please go to
www.profitabilitythinking.com.

PROFITABILITY THINKING

> ➤ Calculate the liquidity, solvency, efficiency and profitability ratios for your business for each of the last three months.
> ➤ Is there a trend in either of the liquidity ratios you calculated that creates a concern in your mind regarding future cash availability?
> ➤ Based on their ratios, are the trends for the amounts you have invested in accounts receivable and inventory heading in the right direction?
> ➤ Is your accounts payable greater than your accounts receivable? Are there steps you can take to create that situation without hurting your relationships with your customers or suppliers?
> ➤ Create a plan to manage each of these ratios and bring the problematic ones back into line.

What are Your Business's Metrics?

Please calculate the following ratios for your business for each of the last three months:

Current ratio	_____	_____	_____
Quick ratio	_____	_____	_____
Average collection period	_____	_____	_____
Average days inventory	_____	_____	_____

Do you see any trends? Are there any problem areas that need attention?

Notes

_____

_____

_____

_____

_____

_____

_____

_____

_____

_____

_____

_____

_____

_____

_____

_____

Notes

_____

_____

_____

_____

_____

_____

_____

_____

_____

_____

_____

_____

_____

_____

Profitability Thinking

Chapter 8
The Cash Flow Statement and Creating a Cash Flow Budget
Pre-Chapter Summary

1. This chapter includes:
- ➤ The formula for cash flow
- ➤ The contents of a Statement of Cash Flows
- ➤ Creating a cash flow budget

2. A profitable business that doesn't have the cash to pay its bills will need to do things that hurt profitability to raise cash, or in a worst case, go bankrupt. When your business has its cash flow squared away, it can be more effectively managed for profitability.

3. The statement of cash flows (also known as the cash flow statement) shows the sources and uses of cash in your business, and is for the same period of time as the income statement such as a month, a quarter or a year. It shows changes in cash from operations, investment activities and financing activities.

4. The formula for cash flow is:

       Profit
- + Depreciation/Amortization (cash from operations) (add back non-cash expense)
- ± Inventory change (cash from operations) (inventory increase means cash decrease)
- ± Accounts Receivable change (cash from operations) (accounts receivable increase means cash decrease)
- ± Accounts Payable change (cash from operations) (accounts payable increase means cash increase)
- ± Fixed Asset change (cash from investing activities) (fixed asset increase means cash decrease)
- ± Debt Obligations (cash from financing activities) (debt increase means cash increase)
- = Cash Flow

5. The contents of a cash flow statement are:
> ➢ Cash from Operations - Day to day operation of the business
> ➢ Cash from Investing Activities - Mostly investments in property, plant and equipment
> ➢ Cash from Financing Activities - Issuing and payment of debt and stock, and payment to owners

6. Creating a cash flow budget is a basic part of business planning. It is a projection of cash inflows and outflows that allows you to plan cash balances in advance, reducing unpleasant cash surprises, and minimizing the chances you will have to borrow money or factor receivables to raise cash to cover expenses.

7. PROFITABILITY THINKING
> ➢ Create a cash flow budget for your business for the next six months.
> ➢ What information about your cash flow does this reveal?
> ➢ Do you have adequate cash coming in to pay your bills without borrowing?
> ➢ Do you have adequate cash coming in to engage in marketing or business building activities?
> ➢ What are your plans for improving your cash flow? The next chapter has 50+ ideas that may help you.

Profitability Thinking

Chapter 8
The Cash Flow Statement and Creating a Cash Flow Budget
The Life Blood of Profitability Thinking

In a book about using your financials to make more profitable business decisions, the chapters about cash flow, cash flow budgeting and cash flow management techniques would have to be considered the Main Event. A profitable business that doesn't have the cash to pay its bills will need to do things that hurt profitability to raise cash, or in a worst case, go bankrupt. When your business has its cash flow squared away, it can be more effectively managed for profitability.

If your business has its cash flow in order, it will be able to take advantage of trade discounts because it has the cash. It won't have to borrow money or factor receivables to raise cash. It will be able to invest in initiatives to create new business because it has the cash. And having cash will allow your business's management to feel more confident asking for pricing and standing firm because they aren't terrified that losing the sale will be the event that finally pushes the business over the edge.

In this chapter and the following one, we'll start by going over the cash flow statement to improve your basic knowledge about cash flow, review cash flow budgeting and cover a great many tactics and strategies that can improve your cash situation.

The Statement of Cash Flows

The statement of cash flows (also known as a cash flow statement) shows the sources and uses of cash in your business and is for the same period of time as the income statement such as a month, a quarter or a year. It shows changes in cash from operations, investment activities and financing activities. Sources of cash can be operations, new loans, issuing stock, or sale of facilities, plant and equipment. Uses of cash can be operations, dividends, loan repayment, stock repurchase, or purchase of facilities, plant and equipment.

You may recall from the chapter about finance basics, the formula for cash flow can be expressed as

> **Profit**
> + **Depreciation/Amortization (cash from operations) (add back non-cash expense)**
> ± **Inventory change (cash from operations) (inventory increase means cash decrease)**
> ± **Accounts Receivable change (cash from operations) (accounts receivable increase means cash decrease)**
> ± **Accounts Payable change (cash from operations) (accounts payable increase means cash increase)**
> ± **Fixed Asset change (cash from investing activities) (fixed asset increase means cash decrease)**
> ± **Debt Obligations (cash from financing activities) (debt increase means cash increase)**
> = **Cash Flow**

Below is an example of a statement of cash flows.

XYZ Company		
Statement of Cash Flows for Period Ending December 31		
Cash Flow from Operations		
Net Income from Income Statement	196,800	
Accounts Receivable Increase	(50,000)	
Inventory Increase	(10,000)	
Accounts Payable Increase	20,000	
Prepaid Expense Increase	(5,000)	
Depreciation	13,272	
Net Cash Flow from Operations		165,072
Cash Flow from Investing Activities		
Equipment Purchase	(10,000)	
Net Cash Flow from Investing Activities		(10,000)
Cash Flow from Financing Activities		
Increase in Long-Term Debt	50,000	
Net Cash Flow from Financing Activities		50,000
Net Increase (Decrease) in Cash		205,072
Cash at the Beginning of the Period		75,000
Cash at the End of the Period		280,072

Profitability Thinking

Some of the things you can see from the cash flow statement example are:

> ➤ The business started the year with $75,000 in cash, had an increase in cash of $205,072 and ended the year with $280,072 in cash.
> ➤ The net income for the period was $196,800, but the increase in cash was $205,072. This further illustrates that profit does not equal cash.
> ➤ The biggest use of cash came from a $50,000 increase in accounts receivable. This should be looked into immediately.
> ➤ The inventory increased $10,000, also a use of cash. This should be investigated as well.
> ➤ Accounts payable increased which may mean the business is holding on to cash longer. That's a good thing, as it increased cash $20,000.

Doing a simple analysis of your cash flow statement can lead you to issues that may need to be addressed. Reading this report monthly will help you understand where your cash is increasing and decreasing.

The Contents of a Statement of Cash Flows

There are three sections to the statement of cash flows: Cash from operations, cash from investing activities and cash from financing activities. The explanations below describe the changes in cash during an accounting period. Contents of a statement of cash flows might include the following and can include more.

> ➤ **Cash Flow from Operations - This is the change in cash created by the day to day operation of the business. It begins with net income from the income statement and is then adjusted by a number of items, as you can see below. Walking through these adjustments should help you understand why profit is not the same thing as cash.**
>> o **Net Income from the Income Statement (Profit) - The statement of cash flows starts with the profit (or loss) from the same accounting period such as a month, quarter or year. However, since profit does not necessarily equal cash, the cash flow statement adjusts net income amount up or down to account for actual cash inflows and outflows.**

- Change in Accounts Receivable - When you sell an item on credit to a customer, the amount of that sale becomes a receivable and remains a receivable until cash is received for its payment. The sale has been booked on the income statement as revenue for the period, but the cash might not have been received yet. If the amount owed to your business by customers increases for the period, an adjustment needs to be made to account for the fact that there were sales and income shown on the income statement but not a commensurate amount of cash received. Therefore, an increase in accounts receivable during the period is a use of cash and is listed as a negative number in the cash flow statement. Conversely, if the accounts receivable account decreases during the period, then you received cash from customers in excess of revenue from sales for the period. That extra cash is shown in the cash flow statement as a positive number, showing the change as a source of cash.
- Change in Inventory - An increase in inventory during the period shows that you have invested more in inventory than was recorded as cost of goods sold on the income statement. To account for this investment in inventory, an increase in inventory is a use of cash and is shown as a negative number in the cash flow statement. However, if your inventory decreased for the period, then you have booked cost of goods sold expenses during the period for which there was not a commensurate amount of cash invested in inventory. Accordingly, that is considered a source of cash and is shown as a positive number in the cash flow statement.
- Change in Accounts Payable - When you buy from a supplier on credit, that amount becomes a payable and will remain so until it is paid with cash. Just as with changes in accounts receivable on the asset side, changes in accounts payable also need to be accounted for, only in the opposite direction. If your accounts payable for the period increased, that means you have booked expenses that decreased profits on the income statement but have not paid for them with a commensurate amount of cash. Therefore an increase in accounts payable during the period is a source of cash and is shown as a positive number in the cash flow statement. A decrease in accounts payable for the period means you made cash payments in a greater amount than your booked expenses on the income statement. Consequently, that is a use of cash and is shown in the cash flow statement as a negative number.
- Change in Prepaid Expenses - Prepaid expenses are expenses such as insurance that have value over a period of time, but are not expensed all at once. In the case of insurance, it is typically paid for in its entirety up front, but expensed monthly over the life of the policy. Accordingly, the amount of expense doesn't equal the cash paid for it until the end of the policy. That being said, an increase in prepaid expenses during the period is a use of cash as your cash outflow exceeded the expenses for these items in your income statement for the period. As a use of cash, it is shown as a negative number in the cash flow statement. Conversely, if your prepaid expenses decrease for the period, then you have recognized expenses in your income statement that exceed your payment in cash for these items. As such, it is shown as a source of cash and is shown as a positive number in the cash flow statement.

- o **Depreciation** - Depreciation is a non-cash expense. It is recognized on the income statement as an expense for the partial use of a fixed asset over a portion of its economic life. But the asset may have been paid for with cash long ago. As such, the amount of the expense recognized on the income statement needs to be added back in the cash flow statement and is shown as a positive number.
  - o **Amortization** - Amortization is the depreciation of intangible assets such as goodwill, patents or copyrights over the life of the asset. They typically exist because a company purchased them and recognized them as a depreciable asset on the balance sheet. As the intangible assets are amortized (depreciated), it shows up as a non-cash expense in the income statement. Because it is a non-cash expense, it is added back in the cash flow statement and is shown as a positive number.
- ➢ **Net Cash Flow from Operations** - Starting with the profit from the income statement and adjusted as described above, the end result is the net cash flow from operations.

- ➢ **Cash Flow from Investing Activities** - Cash flow from investing activities shows the investment in or disposal of capital assets, such as property, plant and equipment. An investment in a capital asset is considered a use of cash and is shown as a negative number in the cash flow statement. The disposal of a capital asset is considered a source of source of cash and is shown as a positive number in the cash flow statement.
  - o **Purchase or Sale of Property, Plant and Equipment** - As described above, if a long term, or capital asset is purchased, that amount is a use of cash is shown as a negative number in the cash flow statement. The disposal of a capital asset is a source of cash and is shown as a positive number in the cash flow statement. If the amount of money necessary to pay for the asset is borrowed, the purchase is still a use of cash with the source of cash being recognized in the financing activities section of the cash flow statement reflecting the debt incurred.
- ➢ **Net Cash Flow from Investing Activities** - Typically this section of the cash flow statement is a use of cash and will show a negative number reflecting a decrease in cash to support this activity.

- ➢ **Cash Flow from Financing Activities** - Financing activities refers to the raising and repaying of capital (cash) from debt and equity sources, as well as distribution of profits to equity sources (owners).
  - o **Change in Short-Term and Long-Term Debt** - Capital (cash) is increased from the issuance of debt and decreased from the repayment of debt. So when you borrow money, that is considered a source of cash and is shown as a positive number on the cash flow statement. When debt is repaid, it is a use of cash and is shown as a negative number on the cash flow statement.

- Share Issues and Repurchases - When your company issues stock and is paid for it, that cash is considered a source of cash and is shown on the cash flow statement as a positive number. When money is paid for shares to be repurchased, that is considered a use of cash and is shown as a negative number on the cash flow statement.
- Dividends Paid - Owners of the business are typically paid in the form of dividends. This payment is a use of cash and is shown in the cash flow statement as a negative number.
- **Net Cash Flow from Financing Activities** - Like the other sections, the increases and decreases of cash from financing activities is netted out to show whether the financing activities of the business increased cash or decreased cash.

Creating a Cash Flow Budget

Later in this book there is a chapter about business planning, and cash flow budgets are a part of that chapter. However, I wanted to cover cash flow budgeting now because this chapter and the next are all about cash flow and ways to manage it.

Creating a cash flow budget is a basic part of business planning. It's a projection of cash inflows and outflows that allows you to plan cash balances in advance, reducing unpleasant cash surprises, and minimizing the chances you will have to borrow money or factor receivables to raise cash to cover expenses. Cash flow budgets are typically created for monthly time periods, but can be created for weekly or even daily time periods. Creating a cash flow budget will make your business life better because you'll have confidence about where the cash to run your business is coming from and that it will be adequate. In order to create a cash flow budget, you will need the following:

- A sales forecast
- An inventory plan to support the sales forecast
- The average collection period for your receivables
- The percent of sales that are cash sales
- The bad debt expense as a percent of credit sales
- When loan payments and taxes are due
- An estimate of the timing of each of your monthly expenses
- The timing of any major purchases

What follows is an example of what a cash flow budget looks like. As you can see, it takes all of the activities that either create cash inflows or cash outflows, and projects them into the future. In the case of the cash flow budget below, I took the raw material and merchandise inventory purchases and based them off of the current month's sales to account for a 30 day supply of inventory and a 30 day average payable period to pay the bill for the inventory. In the case of accounts receivable, I factored in a 2% bad debt expense and then based the

Profitability Thinking

collection on the previous month's non-cash sales to account for a 30 day collection period. I also paid the commissions based on previous month's total sales. (I hid December total sales of $120,000 of which $20,000 were cash sales so you don't see them, but the January accounts receivable and commissions were based of the hidden figures in the spreadsheet).

In the example business's cash flow budget, you can see that:

➢ Some months were cash negative and some cash positive.
➢ The business borrowed $75,000, paid back a $50,000 loan and also made a $50,000 capital purchase of equipment.
➢ The owner was withdrawing $10,000 per month.
➢ Normal operating expenses stayed fairly consistent between $88,000 and $96,000 each month.
➢ If the business hadn't managed the timing of its borrowing, loan payments and capital purchase, it could have found itself in a negative cash position. Projecting future cash flow allowed the company to avoid having a cash flow problem. Even so, the business in the example is playing it very close with its cash situation. It starts each month with a $25,000 - $50,000 cash balance facing normal monthly operating expenses of about $90,000 and an owner's withdrawal of $10,000. As little as a one week delay in collecting receivables could put the business in a negative cash position.

Using a tool like this will help you manage your business. In the next chapter, we'll cover more than 50 ways to improve your cash flow.

For a free cash flow budget template like the one below, go to www.profitabilitythinking.com.

XYZ Company Cash Budget	JAN	FEB	MAR	APR
Cash Beginning Balance	**50,000**	**30,620**	**27,830**	**53,150**
Cash Inflows				
Total Sales	110,000	120,000	100,000	90,000
A / R Collections (98% previous)	98,000	98,000	112,700	83,300
Cash Sales	10,000	5,000	15,000	10,000
Loan Proceeds	25,000			50,000
Other Cash Injection				
Other Cash Inflow				
Total Cash Inflows	**133,000**	**103,000**	**127,700**	**143,300**
Available Cash Balance	**183,000**	**133,620**	**155,530**	**196,450**
Cash Outflows				
Purch Raw Materials (20% of current)	22,000	24,000	20,000	18,000
Purch Merchandise (10% or current)	11,000	12,000	10,000	9,000
Purchase				
Purchase				
Wages and Salaries	25,000	25,000	25,000	25,000
Commissions (5% previous)	6,000	5,500	6,000	5,000
Benefits and Taxes	5,580	5,490	5,580	5,400
Advertising	5,000	5,000	5,000	5,000
Accounting and Legal	200	3,200	200	200
Bank Service Charges	200	200	200	200
Credit Card Fees	100	100	100	100
Delivery Charges	1,500	1,500	1,500	1,500
Insurance	2,000			
Interest	1,000	1,000	1,000	1,000
Memberships and Meetings			5,000	
Office and Operations Supplies	1,000	1,000	1,000	1,000
Rent	10,000	10,000	10,000	10,000
Taxes				5,000
Travel and Auto	800	800	800	800
Utilities and Telephone	1,000	1,000	1,000	1,000
Other				
Other				
Subtotal	**92,380**	**95,790**	**92,380**	**88,200**
Loan Principal Payment	50,000			
Capital Purchases				50,000
Owner's Withdrawal	10,000	10,000	10,000	10,000
Subtotal	**60,000**	**10,000**	**10,000**	**60,000**
Total Cash Paid Out	**152,380**	**105,790**	**102,380**	**148,200**
Monthly Change in Cash	**(19,380)**	**(2,790)**	**25,320**	**(4,900)**
Cash End of Month	**30,620**	**27,830**	**53,150**	**48,250**

Profitability Thinking

Test Your Knowledge

Does an increase in accounts receivable increase cash or decrease cash?

_____

Does a decrease in inventory increase cash or decrease cash?

_____

Does an increase in accounts payable increase cash or decrease cash?

_____

For answers, please go to **www.profitabilitythinking.com**.

PROFITABILITY THINKING

➢ **Create a cash flow budget for your business for the next six months.**
➢ **What information about your cash flow does this reveal?**
➢ **Do you have adequate cash coming in to pay your bills without borrowing?**
➢ **Do you have adequate cash coming in to engage in marketing or business building activities?**
➢ **What are your plans for improving your cash flow? The next chapter will offer 50+ ways to improve your cash flow. Try to find two that apply to your business and implement them immediately.**

Notes

_____

_____

_____

_____

_____

_____

_____

_____

_____

_____

_____

_____

_____

_____

Chapter 9
50+ Ways to Improve Cash Flow
Pre-Chapter Summary

1. This chapter includes:
  - The relationship between accounts receivable and accounts payable
  - Nine strategies for improving accounts receivable collections
  - Seven strategies for improving accounts receivable collection times
  - The Accounts Receivable Aging Report
  - Four ways to improve accounts payable cash outflow
  - The Accounts Payable Aging Report
  - Improving inventory management
  - 10 ways to improve sales revenue and margins as a way to increase cash flow
  - 21 ways to decrease expenses
  - Borrowing and factoring

2. In this chapter cash flow improvement strategies are broken down into eight types of activities. They are:
  - Improve collection and collection times of accounts receivable
  - Improving terms and times of accounts payable
  - Improving inventory management
  - Increasing sales
  - Increasing margins
  - Decreasing Expenses
  - Borrowing
  - Factoring

3. Improving your collection and collection times of your accounts receivable, and creating as much time as possible to pay your accounts payable without harming your relationships with your suppliers and creditors are fundamental to improving your cash situation.

4. Late paying customers and customers who don't pay can leave your business at risk of being short of cash. So can your delays in billing your customers. This chapter covers ways of improving timely collection.

5. If your business offers its customers credit terms to purchase your product or service, then keeping track of how old your accounts receivable balances are is an important part of managing your cash flow and collecting the money owed to you.

The accounts receivable aging report shows the age of your receivables and whether your customers are paying per the terms agreed to.

6. Just as you expect your customers to pay you on time, your suppliers expect to be paid on time as well. One way to manage this is by having an accounts payable aging report, which will show you how many bills are coming due, for what amount and if your suppliers are being paid.

7. A basic way to monitor inventory by item is called turnover analysis. This takes the in stock count of an item and divides it by an average usage to come up with an inventory level in the form of days of supply. The days of supply can then be used as a benchmark for ordering inventory.

8. The real cost of over using a line of credit is not the interest and other costs, it's in not making the hard decisions that would improve your operating cash flow.

9. PROFITABILITY THINKING
- ➢ Review the roughly 50 ideas to improve cash flow that were presented in this chapter and find two that fit your business well. Start today to implement them. After you have done that, find two more. Cash flow management is not passive. Take action.
- ➢ If you don't currently create and review a receivables aging report and a payables aging report on a weekly basis, do so this week.
- ➢ If you don't already have them created on a monthly basis, have your accountant or bookkeeper prepare average collection period, average days of inventory on hand, accounts receivable to sales and inventory to sales metrics this month. If you have your financial information, it's also fairly easy to do this yourself.

11. What are your business's metrics? Please calculate these metrics for your business for the last three months.

Average collection period   _____ _____ _____

Average days of inventory on hand   _____ _____ _____

Accounts receivable to sales ratio   _____ _____ _____

Inventory to sales ratio   _____ _____ _____

What is the value of credit accounts past due?   _____

What is the value of credit accounts greater than 90 days?   _____

Chapter 9
50+ Ways to Improve Cash Flow
Accelerating Profitability Thinking

Now that you understand the cash flow statement and cash flow budgeting, the next step is to find ways of improving your cash situation in an ongoing basis. I have broken cash flow improvement strategies into eight types of activities. They are:

> ➤ Improving collection and collection times of accounts receivable
> ➤ Improving terms and extending times of accounts payable
> ➤ Improving inventory management
> ➤ Increasing sales
> ➤ Increasing margins
> ➤ Decreasing expenses
> ➤ Borrowing
> ➤ Factoring

Not every strategy will apply to your business, but many will. Applying these strategies in a systematic and disciplined way should improve your cash situation and allow you to focus your management activities toward profitability.

The Relationship Between Accounts Receivable and Accounts Payable

Improving your time to collect as well as your ability to collect your accounts receivable without harming relationships with your customers, while creating as much time as possible to pay your accounts payable without harming your relationships with your suppliers and creditors are fundamental to improving your cash situation. These are what we will cover first.

If your sales are stable and customers owe you less than you owe your suppliers, then your customers are paying your business's bills. But if your customers owe you more than you owe your suppliers, the difference is an added investment you will need to make in the business as you have not yet received the cash from your customers needed to pay your suppliers. Therefore, the first order of business is to shorten your average collection period, reduce your uncollectible accounts, and extend your payment times without hurting your relationships with your customers and suppliers, or damaging your credit rating.

Nine Strategies for Improving Accounts Receivable Collections

There is one thing worse than not having a customer and that's having a customer who doesn't pay. Here are nine strategies that if applied in a disciplined manner, can minimize the likelihood of this unfortunate event happening to your business.

> ➢ Do credit checks on all new customers to whom your business sells on credit. Do this without fail. If your new customer is late pay, no pay or BK, then your customer will need to pay at time of sale or service. This can be by check or credit card (more on this in the next segment), but get paid up front.
> ➢ If your existing customers start to fall into the late pay category, negotiate with them to fix the problem or start collecting some or all of the money up front. This may be hard, but not as hard as not getting paid.
> ➢ Limit the dollar amount or number of invoices that new customers can run up. Once they have a payment history with you, then you can allow them more credit.
> ➢ Establish clear payment terms and get it in writing. Have your terms prominently posted on your sales and billing documents. Have the customer initial next to the payment terms section of the sales document. This might be useful later, if the customer claims he didn't understand the payment terms.
> ➢ Have a credit policy. A credit policy is nothing more than a set of rules that apply to your issuance of credit to your customers. This prevents having to make new decisions with each customer. It also allows you to point to your credit policy if a customer objects to the terms you set. It isn't you, it's the policy. Any exceptions to the policy must be approved by a senior officer and then don't make exceptions.
> ➢ Get up-front and ongoing payments on long projects to limit your exposure and alleviate cash flow strains that not getting paid until the end of the project might cause your business.
> ➢ If a customer is late (past 30 days), don't wait to address the problem. Send a friendly late notice after the first billing cycle and then friendly phone calls after that. Don't wait for several months to do something about it. These efforts can and should be friendly so as to keep the customer, but it is your money. So be persistent in escalating steps to work something out with your customer.

Profitability Thinking

> ➤ When all else has failed, don't be afraid to sue. Don't make it personal or let it distract you from the operation of your business. Suing is just another collection method. But it is your money so don't be afraid to go after it.
>
> ➤ The older your receivables are, the less collectable they become. Prompt collection not only improves your cash flow, it reduces the likelihood that the receivable will become uncollectable. In the next section, we'll explore some strategies for improving collection times.

Seven Strategies for Improving Accounts Receivable Collection Times

Late paying customers can leave your business at risk of being short of cash. So can your delays in billing your customers. So here are seven simple strategies that if done in a disciplined way, will reduce the time from sale of the product or service to having cash in the bank. Not every strategy applies to every business, but check and see how many might be used in your business.

> ➤ Accept credit card payments to get paid sooner. You may have to pay a fee to offer this to customers, but you may find it worthwhile because you'll have your cash faster. Doing this might create enough cash to allow you to take trade discounts or avoid incurring interest on borrowed money. The benefit to customers is that they may be able to use the 20+ days they have to pay the credit card in full on top of the 30 days you gave them. This extends their time to pay without harming your cash flow. As an aside, you can do the same thing with your payables. More on that later.
>
> ➤ If you have a mobile sales or service team, accept mobile credit card payments from smart phones. As they say, there's an app for that. Mobile payment facilitates getting your cash a couple of days sooner, eliminating the delay caused by waiting to process the transaction in the office. Shop service providers as costs vary.
>
> ➤ Get invoices out to customers daily at time of shipment or the time the service is rendered. If you wait until the end of the week, or worse the end of the month to send invoices, you've added to your collection period and decreased the available cash to operate your business.
>
> ➤ Process your orders more quickly. If you have inventory on hand, but are taking anything longer than 24 hours to process and ship an order, you're delaying cash coming into your business. The inventory is there and paid for. The sooner you ship and bill, the sooner you will have cash. As an added benefit, creating this level of service would likely make doing business with your company more attractive to customers.

> Set up a minimum invoice amount. Smaller invoices must be paid at time of sale or service, possibly with a credit card. This not only gets your cash quicker, it eliminates the expense of billing the customer.

> Offer trade discounts for early payment. Typically this is a one or two percent discount on the invoice amount if your customers pay in 10 days or less. As with credit cards, there is an expense to this but you will have your cash sooner with the benefits of being able to take your own trade discounts with your suppliers, pay your bills on time, avoid interest and penalties, and not having to factor receivables. There is also the ability to do marketing and advertising that having cash facilitates. Just make sure that if the customers take the discount, they actually pay in 10 days. Some customers will try to take the discount even though they took 30 days to pay.

> Have payments go to a PO box or lock box instead of your office. This can speed up collections by a day or two. How much is a day of sales worth?

The Accounts Receivable Aging Report

If your business offers its customers credit terms to purchase your product or service, then keeping track of how old your accounts receivable balances are is an important part of managing your cash flow and collecting the money owed to you. As we've discussed, the longer your customers take to pay, the more you have to invest to operate the business until payment is finally received. The accounts receivable aging report shows the age of your receivables and whether your customers are paying per the terms agreed to. The following is an example of an accounts receivable aging report.

XYZ Company Accounts Receivable Aging Report							
Customer	0-10 Days	11-30 Days	31-60 Days	61-90 Days	91-120 Days	> 120 Days	Total
ABC Corp	5,000	5,000		2,000			12,000
DEF Corp	-	15,000	5,000				20,000
GHI Corp	5,000						5,000
JKL Corp	-	25,000		3,000			28,000
MNO Corp					5,000	5,000	10,000
PQR Corp	5,000	5,000		10,000			20,000
STU Corp		25,000	5,000				30,000
Total	15,000	75,000	10,000	15,000	5,000	5,000	125,000
Percent of Total	12.0%	60.0%	8.0%	12.0%	4.0%	4.0%	100.0%

As you can see, the above example business has seven customers that have receivables outstanding totaling $125,000. This company offers 2% 10, Net 30 credit terms to its customers. That is, they offer a 2% discount for customers who pay in 10 days or less and all payments are to be received within 30 days.

At this point, 12% of the receivables are eligible for the 2% discount and 72% are within the payment terms set at time of sale. That means 28% of the payments are late! And 8% of the receivables, all owed by one customer, are past 90 days and are likely uncollectable. This business is likely to have cash flow difficulties and may need to borrow to pay its bills.

If your customers buy on terms, a report of this type should be examined weekly. Seeing collection problems when they are starting allows you to take corrective action before cash flow problems start. If it's one customer, the late problem can be addressed with that customer, but if it's multiple customers, then examining your collection efforts and credit policy are definitely in order.

As a reminder from a previous chapter, you can calculate the average age of your receivables with the average collection period formula. The calculation is

Current Accounts Receivable Balance / (Annual Sales / 360) = Average Collection Period.

Also, the accounts receivable to sales ratio calculation is

Accounts Receivable / Monthly Sales = Accounts Receivable to Sales Ratio.

For a free tool to calculate your average collection period and accounts receivable to sales ratios, please go to www.profitabilitythinking.com.

Both of these formulas, along with the accounts receivable aging report and the strategies I presented for collecting your accounts receivable should help you get your arms around accounts receivable management and improve your cash flow.

Four Ways to Improve Accounts Payable Cash Outflow

There are strategies that you can use to improve your cash outflow through accounts payable. Sometimes they involve extending payments or payment terms, and sometimes taking trade discounts is appropriate. Here are four strategies to improve accounts payable cash outflows.

- Just as with offering your customers the opportunity to pay by credit card, negotiate with your suppliers to accept credit card payments on a net 30 day basis. That way you will not only get the 30 days from your supplier, but you may get the 20 interest free days your credit card company offers for payment in full. Check with your credit card company about this. Also, and this should go without saying, pay the credit card bill in full and on time to avoid interest and late charges.
- If you are paying cash, ask for credit terms from your suppliers. If a supplier won't offer to bill you, perhaps a competitor will.
- Negotiate discounts for early payment such as 2% 10, Net 30 with your suppliers and take the discount, if you have the available cash on hand to do so. Taking the 2% discount on net 30 billing is roughly a 36% annualized return on investment. A 1% discount on net 30 billing is roughly an 18% return on investment. Rather than give you a formula, here is the concept behind these returns. (As a reminder, 2%, Net 30 means that the terms of your payable with your supplier allows you to take a 2% discount if you pay in 10 days, or you can pay the full amount in 30 days).

If you take 2% off of your invoice by paying in 10 days when you could have paid in full in 30 days, you have received 2% for the 20 days you paid early. You are in fact giving your supplier a 20 day loan for 2% of what you would otherwise owe. If there are 360 days in a year (I know there are 365, but work with me), then there are 18 twenty day periods in a year. 2% * 18 = 36% (slightly more, if you consider compounding).

- If you find yourself in a tight cash situation, you might try probing to see which of your suppliers is more lenient in enforcing their 30 day payment policy. Just as I explained the importance of managing your receivables, so it is with your suppliers. And some are not as diligent as they should be. In a pinch, it's good to know who will not give you a problem if you pay them in 45 days. You should always pay your bills on time as agreed, but if you are having a problem doing so, this might be a way out. Just be careful not to harm your relationships with your suppliers in the process. That can make a bad situation worse.

The Accounts Payable Aging Report

Just as you expect your customers to pay on time, your suppliers expect to be paid on time as well. However, you have to manage your cash to be able to do so. One way to do this is by having an accounts payable aging report. This will show you how many bills are coming due, for what amount and if your suppliers are being paid. Below is an example of an accounts payable aging report.

Profitability Thinking

XYZ Company Accounts Payable Aging Report					
Supplier	0-10 Days	11-30 Days	31-60 Days	> 60 Days	Total
ABC Corp	5,000	5,000			10,000
DEF Corp	-	15,000		5,000	20,000
GHI Corp	5,000				5,000
JKL Corp	-	25,000			25,000
MNO Corp	5,000				5,000
PQR Corp	5,000	5,000			10,000
STU Corp		25,000		5,000	30,000
Total	20,000	75,000		10,000	105,000
Percent of Total	19.0%	71.4%		9.5%	100.0%

As you can see in the above table, the example business has $95,000 in payments coming due in the next 30 days, no bills that are slightly past due, but $10,000 worth of bills are greater than 60 days old. There might be any number of reasons for these overdue payments to suppliers such as disputes about the quality of goods received, but these balances should be investigated. If you buy on terms, a report of this type should be reviewed weekly.

Improving Inventory Management

How fast can your business turn its inventory investment into cash? We've already covered accounts receivable, so the other main question is how much do you have in inventory and how long does it take to sell it. You may recall from the ratios section of the balance sheet chapters, the way you measure average days of inventory on hand is

Current Inventory / (Annual Cost of Goods Sold / 360) = Average Days Inventory on Hand.

Also, the inventory to sales ratio calculation is

Inventory / Current Monthly Sales = Inventory to Sales Ratio.

For a free tool to calculate average days of inventory and inventory to sales ratios, please go to www.profitabilitythinking.com.

The above formulas measure inventory as if it were one product. Your business may have more than one product, in which case some will move faster and some will move slower. Also, some inventory items may have more days of supply on hand and some will have less days of supply on hand. A basic way to monitor inventory by item is called turnover analysis. This form of analysis takes the in stock count of an item and divides it by an average usage to come up with an inventory level in the form of days of supply.

Let's look at two examples. The first takes the in stock quantity and divides by the quantity sold in the last 30 days multiplied by 30 days to get the number of days of supply in stock. In the example, this company's goal is to have 25 - 35 days of supply of each item.

XYZ Company Inventory Turnover Analysis				
Description	Number in Stock	Number Sold in the Last 30 Days	Days of Supply	Action to Take
Item A	90	45	60	Don't buy
Item B	100	22	136	Reduce supply
Item C	20	6	100	Reduce supply
Item D	50	50	30	In tolerance
Item E	20	30	20	Buy more

As you can see from the above table, three of the five items in the report are over the recommended supply, one is at the recommended supply and one is below the recommended supply. Clearly the business has extra cash tied up in inventory that could better be used elsewhere.

In the last example, the days of supply is calculated using the last 30 days of sales to determine the days of supply in stock. However, sales of products can be uneven and 30 days might not give a good indication of what demand for the product really is. Consequently, in the next example, 90 days of sales are used for the calculation. The calculation is in stock supply divided by quantity sold in the last 90 days multiplied by 90 to get days of supply. For simplicity, the days of supply are the same in both the 30 day and 90 day report examples. This is what the 90 day report would look like.

XYZ Company Inventory Turnover Analysis				
Description	Number in Stock	Number Sold in the Last 90 Days	Days of Supply	Action to Take
Item A	90	135	60	Don't buy
Item B	100	66	136	Reduce supply
Item C	20	18	100	Reduce supply
Item D	50	150	30	In tolerance
Item E	20	90	20	Buy more

However, what happens if the items are seasonal? Then the last 30 days or 90 days of sales might be useless because immediate past usage would not be a good indicator of future demand. Using immediate past usage could leave you with inadequate inventory going into the busy season and overstocked once the busy season is over. This is where sales forecasting is needed. There are a number of ways to forecast sales, but two that you might consider are:

> Use your in season usage from the previous year multiplied by whatever level of growth your business experienced over the last year to drive your seasonal merchandise or raw material purchases to build inventory for this year.
> Create an accurate marketing forecast. Talk with key customers to see what their requirements will be going into the next busy season to inform your estimate of future inventory needs.

There are many inventory control and material requirements planning software programs on the market that can help with managing your inventory. In any event, having a system to control inventory is essential to keeping your investment in inventory adequate to fill your customers' orders but not too much where it absorbs capital that could be used elsewhere in the business.

One of the things you can do to reduce the required amount of inventory to fill your customers' orders is to negotiate shorter lead times and smaller lot sizes with your suppliers. If you can get smaller amounts delivered quicker and more frequently, you can reduce your minimum inventory on hand requirements. This can often be accomplished with blanket orders where you set minimum and maximum delivery quantities each month over a period of time, perhaps one year. Remember, blanket orders work better when sales forecasts are reasonably accurate.

Another way to reduce inventory is to compare days of supply requirements with realistic lead times to obtain the items. If your days of supply target is 30 days but your realistic lead time for the item is four days, you might consider reducing your days of supply target to something less than 30 days.

Years ago I spent some time as a worldwide supply chain manger. The company I worked for purchased large quantities of items from China to be delivered to our plant and warehouse in the Midwest. Part of the lead time calculation my planners used was an assumed 30 days from the point the items left the plant in China to when they arrived at our Midwest facility. However, upon investigation, we realized that our time door to door was only 16 days. I requested that the planners change their ordering to remove 14 days of inventory from what we kept on hand. There are opportunities like this in most businesses that sell products.

Finally, be careful with volume discounts. It might be tempting to get 25% off that lot of 500 units, but if you only sell 10 per month, you just tied up cash for four years. Pay the extra cost for the item, including the extra shipping, and have your capital available to pay bills, pay down debt or invest in initiatives to increase sales.

10 Ways to Improve Sales Revenue and Margins as a Way to Increase Cash Flow

Improving sales and margins may seem like an obvious idea to improve cash flow, but some of the strategies that follow may not be so obvious. Here are 10 strategies to use that might increase your sales and improve your margins. Some of these were also covered as ways to improve profitability in a previous chapter.

➢ Suggest related purchases. If you've ever been to a shoe store, bought appliances or been to a restaurant, you know what I'm talking about. In the case of the shoe store, the sales person will try and sell you shoe trees, shoe polish or a belt. In the case of the electronics store, they always try and sell the extended warranty, or the computer or TV set up service. In the restaurant, it's the bottle of wine, appetizers and dessert. In all cases, these are additional sales at very high margins. Most businesses have related high margin products or services to sell. If you don't, what are some items you might consider adding?

➢ Related to selling additional high margin items is up selling to a better product or service with a better margin. When you buy a car, perhaps you'd like the model with a navigation system and eight speaker stereo. How about the model with the performance package for only $5,000 more? How about something as simple as the better grade motor oil when you get your oil changed?

➢ Have a robust spare parts business. Spare parts are more profitable than new products and can continue sales revenue after the initial sale.

> Reward your sales people for up selling and selling related high margin items. Does your compensation system reward selling high margin items so that your sales people are economically aligned with your business's interests? Make it worth the sales person's time to feature products and services that do your business the most good.

> Stop revenue leaks. Diagram your sales process from order to final collection and find where money is falling through the cracks. Likely causes will be sales not turning in an invoice or customers not being charged for additional work. You might find that some of your revenue has been leaking out of your business. Finding it creates cash flow and the benefit drops straight to pre-tax income (net income in our examples).

> Use a daily cash sheet to monitor daily cash inflows and outflows. Make sure that the transactions for the day and the cash sheet balance. For a daily cash sheet template, go to **www.profitabilitythinking.com**.

> For the most part, your current customers are far more valuable than new customers. It's worth investing in their loyalty and keeping in touch with them. It's a lot cheaper to do that than to try and find a new, good customer. Going after new customers and ignoring the current ones is a classic salesperson's mistake. And it loses good customers, profits and cash flow.

> Asking for referrals is an often overlooked and inexpensive source of new customers. If you've done good work for someone, ask for a referral. In many businesses, rewarding existing clients for referring new clients is an acceptable form of building new business.

> Raise your prices. If you haven't raised your prices in several years, it's about time to do so. You may have started in business with low prices that you haven't raised even though you don't need the aggressive pricing anymore. Now you find yourself struggling because you're not charging enough. Find a way to raise your prices while creating the least amount of customer losses. We covered this in the chapter about using breakeven analysis and profit projection.

> Make sure your operation is running within normal capacity limits so that your variable costs are in line. If not, your contribution margin will be less and your cash flow will ultimately be less. What do you need to do to stop paying overtime, expressing shipping component parts and merchandise, etc? Sometimes we just get used to operating in this manner and become numb to its effects.

21 Ways to Decrease Expenses

Is the money you spend necessary for the successful operation of the business? Could expenses be reduced? Look at each of your monthly expenses and determine if it could be eliminated or reduced. Any spending should be necessary and support the core function of the business. Here are 21 ideas to control expenses.

- Renegotiate your lease. As I'm writing this book, the country is in an economic slowdown. There are commercial vacancies everywhere. It's a buyer's market. Take a look at what kind of a facilities deal might be available in the marketplace. Use that as leverage to get your current landlord to reduce your rent.
- If you pay your employees weekly, change to every two weeks. This will allow you to hold on to your cash longer, and reduce the cost and time of processing your payroll.
- Use an outside payroll processing service. Doing this will keep you from being fined by government agencies for turning in your payroll taxes late as well as free you from having to issue W-2s.
- Use an outside bookkeeping service to keep better records so you can gain control of your expenses and your business. You need good information to make good decisions. This book is predicated on that fact.
- Take a look at your service contracts. Is the cost worth the benefit?
- Require management or senior management approval for all overtime worked. Examine why overtime was necessary and take steps to fix the problem.
- Review the transportation costs, express costs and courier costs you pay for. Is there a less expensive way to achieve the same result? Is the same result even necessary or could a lower cost option with less performance be adequate?
- Review every item you get from every supplier. Can the costs be renegotiated? Is there a less expensive alternative supplier?
- Engage in value engineering of your product. Is there a less expensive item to substitute, a less expensive process or a lesser tolerance in the manufacture that will work just as well?
- Use your suppliers expertise to suggest ways of taking cost out of your product.
- If you have the cash on hand, take the trade discount for paying early. We discussed this earlier in the chapter.
- Measure the return on marketing expenses. Did the marketing add enough sales with enough contribution margin to justify the spend? Could it be done differently to produce a greater return next time? For further discussion about this topic, see the chapter about using breakeven analysis and profit projection.

➢ Use cooperative advertising to reduce your marketing expenses. With co-op advertising, your supplier pays for part of advertising expenses that feature their product. Typically the amount they pay is determined by how much you buy.

➢ Require senior management approval of employee expense reports and require backup for those expenses. Question everything that doesn't make sense. Employees will not be tempted to stretch their expense reports if they know they are being scrutinized.

➢ Scrutinize employee mileage reimbursement. Again, if the employees know they are being scrutinized, they will be less likely to try and get reimbursed for miles not driven.

➢ Install light switches that sense motion and turn off lights when there is no motion in the room.

➢ Use voice over internet protocol (VoIP) to make phone calls, saving on monthly phone bills. Compare several service providers as prices can vary widely.

➢ If you purchase regularly from a supplier, negotiate an end of year rebate if you purchase a certain amount of product. Do not buy extra product for that reason, but if you do purchase that amount, the rebate reduces your net costs. Along the same lines, negotiate contracts for things like office supplies with the lowest cost supplier.

➢ If you are absolutely up against it, consider eliminating annual pay and wage increases for a year. Explain to your staff that the reason this was necessary was to save the business.

➢ Re-evaluate coffee service, cable TV service and other lunchroom perks.

➢ Be aware of purchases you make because "the business bought it and I can write it off." Just because you can write it off doesn't mean it's free. The government is in effect subsidizing your purchase by your marginal tax rate, but you are still paying real money for the item purchased. As an example, if your marginal tax rate is 28% and you buy a $1,000 item that you write off, you will receive a $280 reduction in your taxes, but you paid $1,000 for the item. Assuming you expensed the item, you had a net usage of cash of $720. The moral to this story is not to buy things you would not otherwise buy because the business bought it and you can write it off. Consult your tax advisor for guidance on tax issues.

Not all of these strategies will apply to your business and even if they did, you might not want to use all of them. But eliminating unneeded expenses is a key part of cash flow management. My hope is that this list has generated other ideas as you've read it. Knowing what you're spending and why is a business necessity.

Borrowing and Factoring

From time to time you may find it necessary to borrow money to run your business. Managing your business so it doesn't require borrowing to operate on a day to day business will increase your profitability, your liquidity and your ability to sleep at night. Use some of the previous strategies to help your business to operate in this manner. Here are some thoughts about borrowing money to run your business and factoring receivables to get cash.

> ➢ Along the same lines as the opening paragraph in this section, stop regularly using your line of credit to run your business. Certainly there are the interest charges and fees that are associated with using your LOC, but the real cost is in not making the hard decisions that would improve your normal operating cash flow. These are decisions such as laying off an employee, eliminating an employee perk, changing suppliers or eliminating an unprofitable customer.
>
> ➢ Be keenly aware of how much interest charges and other fees associated with borrowing are costing you. It's easy to become complacent and end up like the frog that gets boiled to death one degree at a time.
>
> ➢ If credit is tight and you can't get a loan, you might consider factoring your receivables. Factoring is where you sell a portion of your receivables to someone else for a discount to raise cash. This can be expensive, but it has the benefit of not being a loan, and there is no interest or payment due, although it will reduce your future cash inflow. Factors don't evaluate your credit, they evaluate the credit of your customers whose receivables you are selling. I have read of people who use these services routinely to run their businesses in a tight credit environment. Undesirable as that may seem, if it's that or not having the cash to pay your bills, then factoring looks like a lifeline.

When you get your cash flow situation under control, you can focus your decision making on the profitability of the business. You will not have to pay interest, factor receivables or discount pricing because you need the order for cash flow. You will have the ability to take trade discounts, invest in marketing to build sales and add additional capacity. And...you will sleep better at night.

Test Your Knowledge

What are the eight ways you can improve your cash flow described earlier in the chapter?

1. _____   5. _____

2. _____   6. _____

3. _____   7. _____

4. _____   8. _____

ROFITABILITY THINKING

> ➤ Review the roughly 50 ideas to improve cash flow that were presented in this chapter and find two that fit your business well. Start today to implement them. After you have done that, find two more. Cash flow management is not passive. Take action.
> ➤ If you don't currently create and review a receivables aging report and a payables aging report on a weekly basis, do so this week.
> ➤ If you don't already have them created on a monthly basis, have your accountant or bookkeeper prepare average collection period, average days of inventory on hand, accounts receivable to sales and inventory to sales metrics this month. If you have the financial information, this is also easy to do yourself.

What are Your Business's Metrics?

Please calculate these metrics for your business for the last three months.

Average collection period   _____   _____   _____

Average days of inventory on hand   _____   _____   _____

Accounts receivable to sales ratio   _____   _____   _____

Inventory to sales ratio   _____   _____   _____

What is the value of credit accounts past due?   _____

What is the value of credit accounts greater than 90 days?_____

Notes

_____

_____

_____

_____

_____

_____

_____

_____

_____

_____

_____

_____

_____

_____

_____

Notes

_____

_____

_____

_____

_____

_____

_____

_____

_____

_____

_____

_____

_____

_____

Profitability Thinking

Chapter 10
Creating a Business Plan and Budgets
Planning for Profitability Thinking

One of the positions I've held in my career was that of sales manager. I believe that if a sales manager (or any other manager for that matter) can get his/her sales team to think properly, they will act properly and increase the likelihood that they will be successful. Accordingly, every year I would have my teams create a business plan outlining what their sales volume, lead volume and conversion rate would be, sources of business and how they would develop those sources, how they would deal with customers, and other elements that supplied a roadmap for them to follow to create business success in the coming year.

One year I inherited a successful veteran sales person who was not initially thrilled at the prospect of having to do his required business plan. But when he finally did it, he approached the project in a positive manner and to his amazement, it highlighted a weakness in his business. The specific weakness was that he was not keeping in touch with previous customers. He fixed that issue with his business and gained sales volume because of it.

The moral to the story is that although a business plan is a roadmap for future action and can be a document shown to bankers and investors, one of the primary benefits of having the discipline to do a business plan is that it makes you a better business person. By focusing on the various aspects of your business and market, you better understand what is required to be successful.

Business Success Begins with a Well Thought Out Business Plan

This book is essentially about how to make the numbers generated by your business work for you to create success and profitability. For this reason, I am concentrating most of our time together on the metrics related to your business, how to understand them and what to do about them. However, the metrics do not happen in a vacuum. They happen as a consequence of operating results. We can concentrate on the metrics of the business all day long, but if the operation is flawed, it won't be a happy exercise. To have good operating results, you need a good plan.

The ancient Chinese warrior-philosopher Sun Tzu in his classic book "The Art of War" said that, "The battle is won or lost before it is ever fought." The modern business equivalent of the Sun Tzu quote is that successful businesses create their success with good plans. With a well thought out plan, your business will have its greatest potential for success If you haven't created a business plan, or haven't done one lately, my suggestion is to do one now so you have a good roadmap from which to operate your business going forward, enhance your own business management skills and optimize your chances for success. There are any number of instructions, templates and books for doing so. Many are free.

Elements of a Business Plan

A full blown business plan can be a rather lengthy document. To the extent that you will use it to obtain financing, it will need to be very thorough. The elements of a business plan are:

- ➢ Executive Summary
- ➢ Company Description
- ➢ Marketing Plan
    - o Description of products and services
    - o Target market description, and probable demand for the products and services
    - o Competitive analysis in terms of number of competitors, differentiation, price, quality and service
    - o Sales and promotion plan
- ➢ Operations Plan
- ➢ Management and Organization
- ➢ Business Development Plan
- ➢ Financial Plan and Budgets

Contents of a Business Plan

In this section we'll review each of the elements listed above and provide more detail as to what comprises each. This is only an overview. Full business plans are much more detailed than can be fully explained in the few pages devoted here. My goal is to introduce you to the concepts behind a business plan and the benefits of doing one.

Executive Summary - An executive summary highlights and summarizes key aspects of your business. If there is a purpose outside of creating a roadmap for your business such as applying for a loan, it should be clearly stated in this section. Questions about how much money you are looking for, what the money

Profitability Thinking

will be used for and how the loan will be repaid should be answered in the executive summary. If you're looking for a partner, explain the reasons why the partnership makes sense. The executive summary should be short and concise (1-2 pages), upbeat as to why the business will succeed, and leave the reader interested to learn more.

Company Description - The company description answers the general questions about who, what, when, where, why and how. Here are the elements of this section.

> The name of your business, its address and other contact information.
> The ownership of your business and its legal structure.
> The business's history, stage of development, and present and future plans for your business.
> A description of the products and services offered by your business.
> A description of important strengths and core competencies of your business.
> A description of challenges facing your business.
> A general overview and outlook for the industry in which your business operates.
> How the business has been funded to date, and any amounts of money you are seeking and why.
> If you have a mission statement, or statements of vision and values, this would be a good section in which to include them.

Marketing Plan - A marketing plan covers all facets of how the business goes to market and how it interacts with its business environment.

Description of products and services - A description of products and services will present the products and services you offer, their technical specifications and how they are produced or delivered. Also, their pricing, quality specifications, positioning in the marketplace and what differentiates them - their unique selling proposition.

Target market - This section will define who buys your product or service, what the size of the market is, the geographic area and type of geographic area you're targeting, as well as the demographic you're targeting.

The competitive landscape - The competitive landscape describes your competition, their market share, and their strengths and weaknesses. It also describes the opportunities you have in the marketplace and the threats your competition poses. Finally, the competitive landscape includes barriers to entry that might exist to reduce new competition to your business.

Sales and promotion plan - This section describes how you will go to market and will include a sales forecast. Will you use direct sales, agents and representatives, partnerships, the internet, or some kind of advertising outreach with an inbound call center? It describes your sales costs in terms of commissions and other compensation. It also describes your advertising, collateral and marketing message.

Operations Plan - The operations plan describes how you will run your business on a daily basis. This would include the processes to make your product or deliver your service, the suppliers who sell you materials and merchandise, the logistics of inbound and outbound freight, your inventory control process, your quality control process, your production and purchasing planning, customer service, and any systems, machinery or equipment necessary to run your business. It will also include any processes that might give you a competitive edge.

Management and Organization - In this section you will introduce the key members of your management team and their qualifications to run your business successfully. It will describe how the organization is structured, the roles and responsibilities of each functional area and its manager, the necessary staffing to run the business, and the human resource policies that guide the organization.

Business Development Plan - Where does your plan for this business take it in five years? The business development section of your business plan describes how you are going to get there. What do future sales, market share, profit margins, number and types of products or services, and the size and characteristics of the organization look like five years from now? It describes the milestones you will need to pass and the timeframes in which they will need to be achieved. It will also describe the resources necessary to achieve the goals outlined.

Financial Plan - There are a number of pro-forma financial statements that need to be part of your business plan. Pro-forma simply means an example using estimates. Pro-forma financial statements in this case are projected financial statements using your assumptions for your business. At a minimum, these should include an integrated set of estimated annual financials for two years to include:

- An Income Statement
- A Balance Sheet
- A Statement of Cash Flows
- A Cash Flow Budget
- A Capital Budget
- Breakeven Analysis
- A Sales Forecast
- Marketing Budget

Business Plans are Not Etched in Stone

If you're concerned about the precision of your pro-forma documents, don't be. Budgets and business plans are obsolete about ten seconds after they are published. They are your best estimate at the time given the facts at your disposal. Make them as thorough, accurate and honest as you can. One of the more difficult pro-formas is going to be the cash flow budget, as predicting cash inflows and outflows farther than six months in advance can be problematic.

With your assumptions about sales, margins and various types of expenses, create your various pro-forma documents. With the sheer volume of numbers necessary to create these pro-formas, this may seem like an overwhelming task. However, just fill in the blanks of your templates in the appropriate places. It's analogous to a large jigsaw puzzle. It looks like an overwhelming number of pieces, but if you just fit one piece together with another, it will eventually create the whole picture. To be truthful, doing an integrated business financial plan is easier and certainly more rewarding than a jigsaw puzzle. There are integrated business plan financial templates available on the web. Some are free.

To give yourself the best chance of getting this done in a timely manner, my suggestion is to employ the services of an accountant or very good bookkeeper to help you. You are not an accountant (I'm assuming), so obtain the assistance of a professional to create the documents based on your assumptions, and review them when they are complete.

Once the documents are prepared, spend the time necessary to understand what they mean, their implications and the things that will impact your success. Use the information in this book to help you. The pro-forma financials are the result of the plans and assumptions you put in place in the rest of the business plan. Therefore, review the following in your pro-forma future financial estimates as if they were real financials describing real financial results.

> ➤ Your gross margin percent of sales trends
> ➤ Your various fixed cost percent of sales and trends
> ➤ Your operating income percent of sales and trends
> ➤ Your breakeven point and breakeven trend
> ➤ Your current and quick ratios, and their trends
> ➤ Your accounts receivable and inventory to sales ratios, and their trends
> ➤ Your days of accounts receivable and inventory, and their trends
> ➤ Your increases and decreases in cash
> ➤ Any cash gaps where you're spending more than you're taking in
> ➤ Your marketing expense as a percent of sales

Do you see any problem areas? Are there trends that might be troublesome if they were to materialize in real life? Now is the time to discover them. That way you can fix future problems before they happen. Also, any prospective lenders, investors or partners will spot them if you don't address them.

Actual v Plan

Once you have your pro-forma documents, have reviewed them and understand them, and are happy with the result, it's time to turn these plans into budgets. Budgets are nothing more than guidelines by which to run your business and a yardstick to gauge how well your actual performance is doing compared to your original plans.

As an example, a sales budget is essentially your sales forecast from your business plan. It is a budget because you now have to meet those sales goals to achieve the results intended in your business plan. Every month compare your actual sales results with your budgeted sales results (business plan sales forecast). Did you exceed your budget? If so, you have a favorable variance to plan. If not, you have an unfavorable variance to plan. In either case, it's useful to determine the reason why.

If the result is favorable, what elements of your business are working better than you thought they would to create the favorable variance? Are those reasons sustainable? Can they be increased? By doing this simple analysis, you will better understand your business results and then have the ability to make decisions based on the analysis to improve your results going forward.

Conversely, if the results are unfavorable, what's not working in your business as well as you thought it would? Can this be corrected? Understanding how your business results vary from your plan and then making decisions as a result will improve your management effectiveness, and your business's profitability and cash flow.

Types of Budgets

Just as there is a sales budget to which you can manage your business, there are a variety of other budgets to which you can compare your operating results. Below is a list of budgets against which you might wish to manage your business.

> ➤ **Sale Budget** - These are your sales assumptions and your sales goals against which you can measure actual sales performance. Making sales is the obvious first step in the business process. Are you making enough sales to meet your business plan? If not, how can the situation be corrected. The sooner you fix unfavorable variances to plan, the better your chances of achieving the result your business plan intended.

Profitability Thinking

> **Cash Flow Budget** - We covered this earlier in the book in the chapter about the statement of cash flows and cash flow budgeting. Knowing how you're doing against this budget is essential to avoiding cash flow gaps and cash shortfalls.

> **Margin Percent Budget** - Your gross margin, operating margin, net income margin and contribution margin should all be part of your business plan assumptions. Are you meeting those assumptions? If not, where is the variance? How can it be corrected?

> **Fixed Expense Budget** - You've assumed a level of expenses necessary to operate your business. Are your fixed expenses what you thought they'd be? Were you too optimistic? What can be done to reduce your expenses to meet budget? If the expense doesn't help create additional business and additional profit, you might think long and hard about spending the money.

> **Marketing Budget** - We also covered this earlier in the book in the chapter about using breakeven analysis and profit projection to manage your marketing expenses. Your actual marketing budget should be part of an overall marketing plan that includes the objectives of the plan. Having a marketing plan with a marketing budget in place before you spend any money allows you to manage this expense and improve the effectiveness of planned marketing initiatives.

> **Capital Budget** - If your business requires large investments in property, plant or equipment, create a capital budget designed to support the operation and growth of your business. Planning for the expenses caused by growth and success will allow you to continue the controlled, profitable growth of your business.

Creating a business plan and accompanying budgets will have a direct affect on the success of your business. I will repeat Sun Tzu. "The battle is won or lost before it is ever fought."

PROFITABILITY THINKING

> **If you don't have a current business plan, develop one. It will give you a roadmap from which to run your business and you will become a far more knowledgeable business person for having done so. You will develop a clarity about your business you didn't previously possess.**

> **Make your business plan a living document by updating it regularly and performing variance analysis of the sales, margin, cash flow and expense portions of the plan. That way you can tell if what you thought was going to happen actually did.**

Notes

_____

_____

_____

_____

_____

_____

_____

_____

_____

_____

_____

_____

_____

_____

_____

_____

Notes

_____

_____

_____

_____

_____

_____

_____

_____

_____

_____

_____

_____

_____

_____

_____

Chapter 11
Using Key Performance Indicators
Monitoring Profitability Thinking

The legendary management expert Peter Drucker once said, "What gets measured, gets done." This chapter is about measuring what is important to your business's performance. We might refer to business measurements as financials or internal metrics, but whatever you call them, they are the gauges of your business's success and tools for its management.

In the previous chapters, we reviewed a great many metrics that you can use to manage your business. To review, some of the metrics we covered are listed below.

> ➢ Sales Volume
> ➢ Sales Units
> ➢ Gross Margin
> ➢ Contribution Margin
> ➢ Operating Margin
> ➢ Net Income
> ➢ Net Income Margin
> ➢ Fixed Expenses
> ➢ Fixed Expenses as a Percent of Sales
> ➢ Return on Assets
> ➢ Return on Equity
> ➢ Current Ratio
> ➢ Quick Ratio
> ➢ Account Receivable to Sales
> ➢ Inventory to Sales
> ➢ Accounts Receivable Days to Collect
> ➢ Accounts Payable Days Sales Outstanding
> ➢ Inventory Days on Hand

These metrics and the others we've covered can be very important to your business's success. However, to manage your business effectively and use your time efficiently, you will want to decide which metrics are the most important to your business's success. These are key measurements against which your business must perform well to be successful. They are called Key Performance Indicators (KPIs).

Your business's KPIs should be tied to specific targets which are under your control and actionable. The number of measurements in your group of KPIs should be relatively small to focus attention on what is important and then be organized in a way that they can be viewed conveniently on one report. This report is called a scorecard or dashboard, and efficiently helps you keep in touch with the performance of the business.

Different parts of the organization can have different KPIs. For instance, at the general management level there might be high level measurements and targets such as sales, investments in accounts receivable and inventory, current ratio, fixed costs as a percent of sales, and gross profit margin. If the KPIs are for operations, then metrics and targets about time per service call, product cycle time, reject rates or percent of orders shipped complete might be in order. In customer service, a KPI might be the number of calls answered within one minute against a targeted level of performance.

Notice that in each case, the measurement is quantifiable, is associated with a performance level target and can be influenced by management action. If you can't measure it numerically, or do anything about it or as a result of it, then in most cases keeping track of it serves no purpose.

KPIs or Flying Blind

Have you ever boarded an airplane and looked into the cockpit? What did you see? A group of gauges that the pilot used to fly the plane. The gauges were to the pilot of that airplane what KPIs are to your business. Without the gauges, the pilot wouldn't know how fast the plane was going, at what altitude, in what direction or how much fuel was left. Kind of useful information if you're flying at 35,000 feet in the middle of the night. Without the gauges, the pilot is flying blind. Your KPI gauges may contain different information, but without them you're flying just as blind.

At various points in this book I have mentioned the importance of using detailed, accurate and timely information to help run your business. Having systems and processes to support providing this information is essential. The system and process can be as simple as having an assistant (or you) enter the information from your financials into an Excel spreadsheet that summarizes the information or as complicated as overlaying a financial reporting package to summarize the output of your accounting, MRP and CRM packages. It just needs to be done.

I'm old enough to remember one of the businesses I worked for requiring managers and supervisors to turn in daily hand written worksheets that were then summarized and distributed to the entire company (without e-mail) by noon (this was in the early '80s). It doesn't take complex software to get this done.

As an aside, there are many relatively simple KPI packages available. To see if I have found a KPI system I would recommend, please visit **www.profitabilitythinking.com**.

Key Performance Indicators by Function

KPIs will differ based on whether you're the CEO or the plant manager. Even if you are both the CEO and the plant manager, the hat you're wearing at the moment will define what KPIs you need to look at to be successful. What follows are lists of possible KPIs that might be useful to support the success of typical business functions. These lists are provided as a guide and a thought starter. Whatever the KPIs you choose should be reviewed consistently at appropriate times (daily, weekly, monthly).

General Management

- Gross sales per week
- Gross profit margin
- Operating profit margin
- Net income
- Current ratio
- Quick ratio
- Return on assets
- Return on equity
- Days inventory
- Days accounts receivable
- Number of days cash on hand/burn rate
- Operating cash flow
- Customer satisfaction
- Percent of orders shipped complete
- Percent of orders shipped on time
- Sales volume per FTE (full time employee)

Sales/Marketing

- Number of sales calls made by a salesperson
- Average number of sales calls made per salesperson
- Conversion rate
- Average size of sale/order size
- Gross margin
- Average sales per sales person
- New customers contacted
- Returning customers
- Customers who have purchased in the last 30 days
- Customer satisfaction
- Number of calls answered within one minute
- Order pipeline in number of orders or dollars
- Profitability by product line
- Profitability by customer
- Profitability per salesperson
- Profitability by salesperson
- Response rate per mailing/commercial
- Return on marketing dollars invested

Manufacturing/Supply Chain

- Cycle time (time to manufacture an item)
- Reject rate/quality rate
- Scrap rate
- Number of hours of overtime worked per week
- Hours of temporary workers worked per week
- Time per service call
- Cost per unit
- Orders shipped per day
- Orders shipped on time
- Orders shipped complete
- Number of days of inventory/inventory turn rate
- Lead time between ordering merchandise and receipt of merchandise
- Production rate per hour
- Orders shipped per FTE

As you can see, there are any number of measurements that can be tracked over time. The question is, which are key to your business's or department's success, and what are the targets against which these KPIs are measured. For instance, if one of your key success metrics is sales and you have a target of

$2,000 per day in gross sales, if your sales were $2,200 per day, then you achieved 110% of targeted performance. This seems simple, but having a group of measurements that are key to success, focusing on them consistently and developing plans to improve them over time will yield big results.

Performance against KPI targets can be shared by inter-company e-mail or posting them in the lunchroom as a way of keeping everyone focused on what's important to the success of the business. They can also be used as a carrot to reward success in achieving company goals.

One of the other business experiences I've had was working for a company that changed its dress code monthly based on achieving the organization's prior month's goals. At the time, the company had a dress code of coat and tie. However, if the organization achieved one of its three key goals, you could dress casually on Friday. If two goals were achieved, you could dress casually Thursday and Friday. If all three goals were achieved, you could dress casually all month long. That was one of the most effective ways of engaging employees in a company's success I have ever seen.

PROFITABILITY THINKING

- ➢ **Create key performance metrics and targets to measure the progress of your business in areas vital to its success.**
- ➢ **Create other key metrics and targets for operational areas of your business to measure operational success in that area.**
- ➢ **Create scorecards/dashboards for the business and each operational area that are consistently published at appropriate times (daily, weekly, monthly).**
- ➢ **Share non-confidential KPIs with your business's employees in a way that engages them.**

What are Your Business's Metrics?

What are the three to five metrics that are key to your business's success? What are the targets you would like to see achieved in those areas?

KPI	Target
_____	_____
_____	_____
_____	_____
_____	_____
_____	_____

What are operational areas in your business where KPIs would be useful?

1. _____

2. _____

3. _____

4. _____

Profitability Thinking

Notes

_____

_____

_____

_____

_____

_____

_____

_____

_____

_____

_____

_____

_____

_____

_____

_____

Notes

_____

_____

_____

_____

_____

_____

_____

_____

_____

_____

_____

_____

_____

_____

_____

_____

Profitability Thinking

Chapter 12
Making Your Days Count
Personal Profitability Thinking

In the late 19th century there was an Italian engineer, economist and philosopher named Vilfredo Pareto. He observed that 80% of the land was owned by 20% of the people. Later, he apparently discovered that throughout history in various civilizations, 80% of the wealth was owned by 20% of the people. This phenomena was later dubbed the Pareto principle. The Pareto principle has since been generalized to other areas of life, economics and business, and has come to be known as the 80/20 rule.

In business the 80/20 rule has been used to state that 80% of your sales come from 20% of your customers, 80% of your sales come from 20% of your products, 80% of your sales are generated by 20% of your salespeople or 80% of your profits come from 20% of your customers/products/salespeople. You get the idea. Whether the ratio is 80/20, 80/50 or 75/25, the concept that business results of any kind are not equally distributed has merit.

The results you get from your business efforts are likely not equally distributed either. Some activities you do have much more value to you, your business and your goals than other activities. By focusing on these high value activities, you can create a quantum leap in your results. Let's do a little math to illustrate this point.

Let's assume that you work 40 hours per week (I know entrepreneurs don't usually have that luxury, but work with me) and that your work generates $4,000 per week in income. Now let's assume that 80% of your income comes from 20% of your work. Let's do the math.

The Math of the Pareto Principle

If the income was equally divided by the hours worked, the calculation would be

$4,000 income / 40 hours worked = $100 per hour.

However, the income generated is not equally distributed in reality. In our example, 80% of the income is generated by 20% of the hours worked, which implies that 20% of the income is generated by 80% of the hours worked. So let's compare how much the high value work is worth per hour to how much the low value work is worth per hour. The high value work can be calculated as

($4,000 * 80%) / (40 hours * 20%) = $3,200 / 8 hours = $400 per hour.

Now let's calculate the value of the lower value activities. The calculation is

($4,000 * 20%) / (40 hours * 80%) = $800 / 32 hours = $25 per hour.

As you can see, the high value work on which you spend only 20% of your time is worth 16 times the value per hour as the lower value work on which you spend 80% of your time. Can you see how you might do well to concentrate on high value work? Further, the lower value work is worth a small enough value per hour that it could easily be delegated. So what would happen if you focused 80% of your time on the high value activities and only 20% of your time on the lower value activities. How much would that be worth per week? The calculation is

($400 per hour * 32 hours) + ($25 per hour * 8 hours) = $12,800 + $200 = $13,000 income per week.

Now I can hear you object that the 24 hours of low value activity didn't just disappear. It still has to be done. Fair enough. Delegate it at the pay rate of $25 per hour.

So the new weekly value you are generating can be calculated as

$13,000 - (24 hours * $25 per hour) = $13,000 - $600 = $12,400 income per week.

The additional income created by concentrating on high value activities and delegating some of the low value activities is

$12,400 - $4000 = $8,400 in additional income per week by concentrating on high value activities.

Now I suspect you're thinking that hiring someone for only 24 hours to assist you will require that you spend time training that person and they still wouldn't be able to do these low value jobs as efficiently as you do. OK. Let's hire the person making $25 per hour for a full time 40 hours per week and stipulate that the eight hours per week you spend on low value activities is for nothing more than training and supervising your full time assistant and has no dollar value per hour. The calculation then becomes

($400 * 32) - ($25 * 40) = $12,800 - $1,000 = $11,800 income per week.

So your weekly income went from $4,000 to $11,800 by hiring a full time assistant to do all of your low value work assuming you work on very high value activities 32 hours per week. In the example, you almost tripled your income by concentrating on what has value. You stopped being the chief cook and bottle washer, jack of all trades and master of none, worker running like a hamster on a wheel going nowhere working in your business, and started being a businessperson working on your business finding customers, creating products, networking and finding ways to build your business.

Now I know your situation is likely to be different. The numbers are different and the 80/20 rule might be some other ratio, but I guarantee you that this series of calculations has application in your life and your business to some degree. Probably a significant degree.

Concentrate on High Value Activities

Earlier in this chapter I made reference to a 40 hour work week. We all know that the 40 hour work week is more of an aspiration than a reality. Work seems to have intruded into anything that used to resemble free time, family time or personal time. Our smart phones, PCs at home and tablets have allowed access to work and intrusion by work at all hours of every day. This level of work causes burnout, and destroys inspiration and creativity. Perversely, it can actually take us away from our goals and aspirations.

As I've demonstrated previously, not all work is created equal or provides equal benefit. To reach our goals and get our lives back, we each must ruthlessly concentrate on what's important and concentrate on high value activities. There are four steps to being able to concentrate on high value activities. They are:

> ➢ Decide what's really important and what you really want.
> ➢ Decide on the highest value activities that will get you there.
> ➢ Eliminate low value activities to make room for high value activities.
> ➢ Have the discipline and process to consistently concentrate on high value activities.

Decide What's Really Important and What You Really Want

The celebrity economist Ben Stein once said, "The essential first step in getting what you want out of life is this: Decide what you want." This simple statement is so profound I consider it to be one of the secrets to a good life. Yet very few people have figured out what they want and fewer have what they want firmly fixed in their minds with such clarity that they instinctively act to achieve it on a consistent basis.

So what's important to you? This book is about business, but your answer can be business or non-business. With that in mind, what is the income, goal or other reward to which you aspire? What are your goals for your business? What does outrageous success look like for your business? What are the sales, gross margin, market share, profit, number of customers, number of locations or number of products that would make for this kind of success in your business? In what time frame would you like to see these occur?

There is an acronym in goal setting called S.M.A.R.T. This means that a goal should be:

> Specific
> Measurable
> Actionable
> Realistic
> Time bound

Specific means that your goals should be very clear in your mind. It's better that you write them down.

Measurable means simply that. More sales isn't measurable. Raising my sales from $50,000 per month to $100,000 per month is measurable.

Actionable means there are specific actions you can and need to take to achieve the goal. This means that action is possible and defined.

Realistic means that you have the ability and willingness to do it. Very often an ambitious goal is more realistic than a minor goal because the ambitious goal inspires you to achieve it.

Time bound simply means you put your goal on a clock. If I didn't set a deadline to finish this book, I'd probably still be writing it. So if your goal is to increase your sales from $50,000 per month to $100,000 per month, then you should include a timeframe in which you want to achieve this goal. Accordingly, the goal might be to increase sales from $50,000 per month to $100,000 per month within 24 months. Since that is a long time, perhaps you create a sub-goal to reach $75,000 per month within 12 months.

Step one is knowing what you want, having it be crystal clear in your mind and writing it down.

Decide the Highest Value Activities that Will Get You There

I was at the optometrist getting a new prescription for contact lenses a few months back. The optometrist was in a big box store and was planning on starting her own independent practice. We began talking about her business plans. I'm not sure where in the conversation she said that she planned to do all the bookkeeping and back office work like ordering glasses from the manufacturer herself, but when I heard that I almost fell out of the chair (hard to see the eye chart from the floor). I asked her to think about how much she makes per hour doing eye exams and compare it to how much per hour an assistant would cost her. To me, that calculation was a no brainer. However, she was uneasy with it. She had such pride in what she was about to do, that she wanted to have everything be perfect. Although I admire that kind of pride in running a good business, her business success will hinge on doing eye exams and finding customers. Everything else should be delegated.

What activities are key to achieving your goals? If one of your goals is to increase sales from $50,000 per month to $100,000 per month in 24 months or less, then there are certain activities that will support such an effort. Some of these activities might include:

> - Networking with prospective customers
> - Meeting with customers
> - Meeting with referral partners
> - Doing market research
> - Creating marketing programs and evaluating their results
> - Creating new products
> - Working with a web designer to enhance your website to allow e-commerce
> - Enhancing your operational processes to support more volume with the same infrastructure
> - Hiring a manufacturers' rep to represent you in the marketplace
> - Establishing a business credit line to support added sales
> - Engaging in the professional activities of a practice

You get the idea. Nowhere on that list was there any of what I like to call administrivia, the definition of which is administrative detail that bogs you down and adds no value. The kind of thing the optometrist in my story should delegate, such as bookkeeping and ordering merchandise. What are the high value activities in your business to which you should devote your time? Which are the ones to eliminate, delegate or outsource?

Eliminate Low Value Activities to Make Room for High Value Activities

Time cannot be managed. Time simply is. Activities on the other hand, can be managed. We all have 24 hours in a day. No more. No less. Being effective is about HOW we use the time we have. The great UCLA coach John Wooden once said, "Don't mistake activity for achievement."

Have you ever had a day where you were busy all day long, constantly in motion, but at the end of the day you accomplished nothing and ended up where you started? Silly question! I suspect we've all had that experience. Some of us more than others. So how do we get off the treadmill? Well we've discussed deciding what's important and what our high value activities are. So the next step is to get rid of low value activities to make room for high value activities.

Since you can't create time, the only way to add available time to do something of high value is to stop doing something else of less value. If you want your life to be better and your business activities more profitable, you need to figure out what to stop doing so that you can concentrate on what you should be doing to make your life and business better. I will take that one step further. If you're working 60+ hours per week, you need to figure out what to stop doing so you can work less. You will not be creative and inspired if you're burned out. Sorry, that's just the way it is. It's also no virtue to work yourself into an early grave or miss your children growing up because you wouldn't delegate things that others could do.

Spend the next week logging your activities in 15 minute increments. At the end of the week, start to evaluate what were the time wasters and what were activities that moved you toward your goals. Start ruthlessly eliminating the time wasters and replace them with activities that move you toward your goals. Learn to say no to things that are not high value and will absorb your day. Identify the two or three goals you have for the week or the month, and make sure nothing else gets on your to do list.

And finally a word about e-mail. Although e-mail creates the ability to instantly contact and exchange information with people anywhere in the world, it can consume your day. One way to get control of your e-mail is to not answer e-mails when they arrive. Put an "Out of Office" message on your email stating that "you are currently in a meeting and will answer e-mails from X AM to Y AM and again from X PM to Y PM. If urgent, please call me." Then minimize the program so you can't see it, disabling any audible cues for incoming e-mails. You can even choose to not have e-mails arrive at your inbox until you retrieve them. That way you can create new e-mails without being drawn into newly arrived e-mails sitting in your inbox.

This might seem extreme, but once you see how much time you waste on e-mail, these solutions will make sense.

Have the Discipline and Process to Consistently Concentrate on High Value Activities

I don't know about you, but I have caught myself doing administrivia because it filled time and didn't tax my mind. It's easy to do. For me it was a sign I was getting burned out. Consistently doing high value activities takes discipline and it takes a process, but if done correctly will reduce the likelihood of burnout.

Profitability Thinking

Let's start with the discipline to plan your next day's work before you leave the current day's work and then scrutinizing your plan for low value activities. Spending the time to write a to do list and prioritize the activities, removing any that should be delegated, eliminated or outsourced is a high value roadmap for the next day. Don't just transfer items from your Outlook calendar. Actually write the list down giving it some thought.

Make sure that what you have on your to do list aligns with your goals. If anything doesn't, you have to ask yourself what it's doing there. It's the discipline to only work on high value activities that will create the value in your life and in your business. That really is Profitability Thinking.

Make sure you track how you're doing. It's easy to fall back into old habits. Take the time to write down your successes managing your days and evaluate the days that weren't as effective as you would have liked them to be. Make plans to fix the causes of the ineffective days and keep at it until they are fixed. Like everything in this life, using your time effectively is a choice. So is not using your time effectively. It takes discipline, but it can be done.

One final thought about creating the discipline to do high value activities, and that is to not think about it at all. That's what I do when I go to the gym. If I had to think about when I will go to the gym, I'd never go so I take the decision out of my hands. I have specific days and times I go and it's automatic. If it's Tuesday at 7:30, I'm at the gym...period. No thought involved. Are there high value things in your business that you can make automatic?

PROFITABILITY THINKING

- ➢ Take a few hours and decide what's really important, and what you really want for your life and your business. Write these goals down. Make sure that these goals are Specific, Measurable, Actionable, Realistic and Time bound.

- ➢ Take a few more hours and decide on the highest value activities that will get you to your goals. What are the essential things that you need to do on a consistent basis to make your business the success you would like it to be?

- ➢ Eliminate low value activities to make room for high value activities. Review your week in 15 minute increments and identify the low value activities and time wasters. Ruthlessly eliminate, delegate or outsource them. Make a not to do list. Replace these activities with activities that support what you're trying to do with your business and your life.

- ➢ Have the discipline and process to consistently concentrate on high value activities. Create your next work day before you leave the current work day. Prioritize the next day's activities, eliminating, delegating or outsourcing low value activities. Track your progress so you don't fall back into old habits.

What's Important to You?

Identify three inspiring and aspirational goals for your business. Make them S.M.A.R.T goals. Then create one high value activity to support each.

1. Goal - _____

A.   High Value Activity - _____

2. Goal - _____

B. High Value Activity - _____

3. Goal - _____

C. High Value Activity - _____

Make a list of five low value activities or time wasters that you would do well to get out of your schedule. Then make a plan to eliminate, delegate or outsource them. This is your not to do list.

Low Value Activity 1 - _____

Low Value Activity 2 - _____

Low Value Activity 3 - _____

Low Value Activity 4 - _____

Low Value Activity 5 - _____

Notes

_____

_____

_____

_____

_____

_____

_____

_____

_____

_____

_____

_____

_____

_____

Chapter 13
Putting it All Together
Monitoring Profitability Thinking

The Numbers are Your Ally

If you've read this far, I suspect I don't need to convince you that the numbers are your ally in managing your business more profitably with better cash flow. If you have the proper information, and do some quick math prior to or as a result of your decisions, you will become more effective at managing your business.

I also suspect you may have found all this information a little overwhelming. It needn't be so. Simply create a routine that takes 30 - 60 minutes per week and an hour at the end of the month to check specific metrics important to your business on a consistent basis. Take some time to analyze and evaluate your business initiatives to see if they will accomplish what you intend or are performing as you thought they would. Then consistently use your time on what matters most. That's it. I've just given you some tools and perspective to do that.

This book was never meant to be just another business book to be read and put on a shelf. The concepts, strategies and tools presented in this book are meant to be used to manage your business every day. Every day you have pricing decisions, product and customer decisions, investment decisions, marketing decisions, decisions about paying suppliers and collecting from customers, decisions about what your business will look like in six months or six years, and decisions about how to spend your precious time so your business will prosper. Every day you have the opportunity to make your business better by the decisions you make. Every day you have the opportunity to engage in Profitability Thinking.

You now have tools to change the way you approach your business. The tools presented in this book and summarized in this chapter, and tools that are at **www.profitabilitythinking.com.** You have your accountant and/or your bookkeeper to help you. You have other resources that you have developed along the way. And you have your expertise in your chosen field of business. That's a powerful combination for success. Just like the business owned by my parents' friends, make your business an American success story.

I want to thank you for investing your time in reading this book and learning what it has to offer. I really believe that if you can change a person's skills and thinking at the same time, amazing results can happen. So go make amazing results happen in your business. You have the tools. I wish you well.

The Profitability Thinking Top Ten

What follows is a Top Ten Profitability Thinking list that synthesizes the Profitability Thinking sections from the preceding chapters into a concise list.

1. Make a commitment to read your

> ➤ Income Statement
> ➤ Balance Sheet
> ➤ Cash Flow Statement

monthly at a minimum, and read your

> ➤ Aged Receivables Report
> ➤ Aged Payables Report

weekly at a minimum. These are the basics to get control of your business. Make sure the format of your Income Statement and Balance Sheet have enough detail to identify key areas of your business, and have them presented to you with several sequential months side by side so you can identify trends. Are your margins acceptable and heading in the right direction? Are your fixed costs stable in absolute terms and declining as a percent of sales? Are your inventory, accounts receivable and accounts payable headed in the right direction? Immediately take action to manage those trends as you spot them. This would seem simple, but are you doing it in a disciplined way on a consistent basis? Doing this will improve your profitability and cash flow, and reduce your business risk.

2. Use the tools at **www.profitabilitythinking.com** to create your

> ➤ **Liquidity** (current ratio, quick ratio)
> ➤ **Solvency** (debt to equity, debt to assets)
> ➤ **Efficiency** (accounts receivable to sales, average collection period, inventory to sales, days inventory on hand)
> ➤ **Profitability** (net income percentage, operating income percentage, net income percentage, return on assets, return on equity)

ratios on a monthly basis at a minimum. If your accountant or bookkeeper will do this for you, so much the better. Is there a trend in your liquidity ratios that suggest future cash flow problems? Are your accounts receivable and inventory to sales trending in the right direction? Are your gross margin, operating margin and net income margin acceptable, and trending in the right direction? Use these and other ratios as a guide to manage your business more effectively and with less risk.

3. Know the breakeven point for your business and business units, and how to project profits for them under various pricing, volume, contribution margin, marketing and cost assumptions that you might consider. Knowing this information will help you make better business decisions and avoid costly mistakes because you will understand the likely effects of your pricing, investment and marketing decisions before you make them. With this in mind, test raising your prices as a strategy to improve your contribution margin. Do the profit projections to see which level of pricing and volume will give you the best return.

4. Improve sales and margins by suggesting related purchases. Most businesses have related high margin products and services to sell. If you don't, what are some high margin items you might consider adding? Related to selling additional high margin products and services is up selling to a better product or service with better margins. Have a robust spare parts business. Spare parts are more profitable than new products and can continue sales revenue after the initial sale. Add more value to your product or service and charge for it. Examples might be improving product quality, enhancing product performance or creating a unique feature, improving service levels, better post sales support and better product training. Finally, reward your sales people for up selling, selling related high margin items and spare parts. Make it worth the sales person's time to feature products and services that do your business the most good.

5. Create a cash flow budget for your business for the next six months. A template for one is available at **www.profitabilitythinking.com**. What information about your cash flow situation does your budget reveal? Do you have adequate cash coming in to pay your bills without borrowing? Do you have adequate cash coming in to engage in marketing or business building activities? Take another look at the 50+ cash flow management ideas presented the chapter about improving cash flow and see if you can find two or three you can implement today.

6. Do credit checks on all new customers to whom your business sells on credit. Do this without fail. If your new customer is late pay, no pay or BK, then your customer will need to pay at time of sale or service. This can be by check or credit card. Limit the dollar amount or number of invoices that new customers can run up. Once they have a payment history with you, then you can allow them more credit. If your existing customers start to fall into the late pay category, negotiate with them to fix the problem or start collecting some or all of the money up front. This may be hard, but not as hard as not getting paid. Establish clear payment terms and get them in writing. If a customer is late per terms agreed to, don't wait to address the problem. Send a friendly late notice after the first billing cycle and then friendly phone calls after that. Don't wait for months before doing something about it. These efforts can and should be friendly so as to keep the customer, but it is your money. So be persistent in escalating steps to work something out with your customer.

7. Create a marketing and advertising budget as part of an overall marketing plan determined in advance of any advertising or marketing spend. Use breakeven analysis and profit projection to quantify the required contribution margin necessary to proceed with a marketing spend. Measure the results of every marketing spend you make. Did it create the level of added sales and contribution margin necessary to justify the expense? If yes, repeat. If no, try something else. Unless you measure, you won't know whether your spend was profitable or not. Measure the return on investment of your marketing against alternatives. Just because a spend was profitable doesn't necessarily mean that it was the most profitable of all the alternatives. Always try to increase your marketing return on investment by testing and improving marketing spends to create the maximum return on your marketing investment.

8. If you don't have a current business plan, develop one. It will give you a roadmap from which to run your business and you will become a far more knowledgeable business person for having done so. You will develop a clarity about your business you didn't previously possess. Update your business plan regularly and perform variance analysis by comparing your actual sales, cash flow, margins and expenses with your plan. Are you on track? If not, what is causing the differences? If the variances are favorable, can you increase the activity that caused the favorable variance? If the variances are unfavorable, can they be fixed or do you need to adjust your plan to a new reality?

9. Create key performance metrics for your business and operating units. Then set targets for each of these key performance metrics to measure the progress of your business in areas vital to its success. Create scorecards/dashboards for the key metrics of your business that you and your managers regularly review (daily, weekly, monthly) to ensure that your business is running as it should. Share appropriate non-confidential metrics with everyone in the business so that everyone is working toward the same goals.

10. Take some time soon to decide what's really important to you, and what you really want for your life and your business. Write these goals down. Make sure that these goals are Specific, Measurable, Actionable, Realistic and Time bound. Then decide which are the highest value activities that will get you to your goals. What are the essential things that you need to do on a consistent basis to make your business the success you would like it to be? Ruthlessly eliminate, delegate or outsource low value activities and time wasters to make room for high value activities. Make a not to do list. Replace these activities with activities that support what you're are trying to do with your business and your life. Then create the process and discipline to do these activities consistently.

Notes

_____

_____

_____

_____

_____

_____

_____

_____

_____

_____

_____

_____

_____

_____

_____

_____

Chapter 14
The Profitability Thinking Glossary
The Ideas of Profitability Thinking

This is the Profitability Thinking Glossary. I've included it as a quick reference for 16 terms and concepts used in this book to save you from having to search through the chapters to find them. It's in alphabetical order.

Accrual Accounting v Cash Accounting

There are two types of accounting: cash accounting and accrual accounting. Accrual accounting is typically better than cash accounting because it reflects the economic reality of the business. Cash accounting recognizes income when cash is received and recognizes an expense when an obligation such as a bill is paid. Accrual accounting recognizes income when goods are shipped or a service provided, and recognizes an expense when the business sells a product or takes on the obligation to pay for something. The implication is that **profit does not necessarily equal cash received.**

The reality of accrual accounting means that you not only have to know that your business is profitable, but you also need to know what your cash flow situation is at any point in time. Many profitable businesses have failed because they didn't manage cash flow and had all of their cash tied up in un-spendable assets. You need to manage both cash and profitability.

Accounts Payable Aging Report

Just as you expect your customers to pay you on time, your suppliers expect to be paid on time as well. However, you have to manage your cash to be able to do so. One way to do this is by having an accounts payable aging report. This will show you how many bills are coming due, for what amount and if your suppliers are being paid.

A report of this type should be examined weekly. It will prevent cash flow surprises and preserve supplier relationships by insuring they are paid on time.

Accounts Receivable Aging Report

If your business offers its customers credit terms to purchase your product or service, then keeping track of how old your accounts receivable balances are is essential to managing your cash flow and collecting the money owed to you. The longer your customers take to pay you, the more your company has to invest to operate the business until payment is finally received. The accounts receivable aging report shows the age of your receivables and whether your customers are paying per the terms agreed to.

A report of this type should be examined weekly. Seeing collection problems when they are starting allows you to take corrective action before cash flow problems start. If it's one customer, the late problem can be addressed with that customer. If it's multiple customers, then examining your collection efforts and credit policy is definitely in order.

Balance Sheet

The balance sheet reports a business's financial position at a specific point in time as opposed to over a period of time, usually at the end of the month, the end of the quarter or the end of the year. It shows the business's financial condition at a point in time, but not how it got there. The balance sheet consists of assets which are what the company owns or is owed by others, liabilities which are what the company owes to others, and owner's equity which is what is left over after assets are subtracted from liabilities and represents the owner's investment in the business. Owner's equity is not what the company is worth or what it could be sold for. It's just what is left over, from an accounting point of view, when you subtract liabilities from assets. The equation for this is

Assets = Liabilities + Owner's Equity or Assets - Liabilities = Owner's Equity.

Breakeven Analysis

Breakeven analysis, also called cost/volume/profit analysis, takes information used to create the income statement (P&L) and rearranges it into a different kind of income statement. Its components are sales revenue, variable costs and fixed costs. Sales revenue is revenue after returns and allowances are deducted from gross sales (sales).

Variable costs are costs directly associated with the production and sale of the product or service that increase or decrease with volume such as costs of goods sold (direct labor and materials), sales commissions, delivery charges, sales bonuses, and direct supplies. All of these typically increase and decrease with the level of sales. Total variable costs as a percent of sales should remain relatively constant within the range of sales in which your business typically operates.

Fixed costs are costs which happen whether a product is sold or not, such as rent, insurance, interest on debt, the salaries of office workers, advertising and promotion, computers for the office and utility bills. Fixed costs in absolute terms should remain relatively constant within the range in which your business typically operates.

When you subtract variable costs from sales you get a contribution margin, which is labeled as such because it is the portion of a sale that contributes to the payment of fixed costs and then to profit. Contribution margin is usually expressed as a percentage of sales or in dollars per unit, and is relatively constant within the range in which your business normally operates.

The key concept in breakeven analysis is that you start every month in the hole for the amount of your monthly fixed costs. You then apply the contribution margin from sales during the month against the fixed costs to fill that hole until you sell enough to breakeven. Once you breakeven, the contribution margin on additional sales is applied to profit. To calculate your breakeven, divide your fixed costs by your contribution margin percent which can be expressed as

Breakeven Volume = Fixed Costs / Contribution Margin percent.

To calculate your breakeven in units, divide your fixed costs by your contribution margin percent by your product price which can be expressed as

Breakeven Units = Fixed Costs / Contribution Margin percent / Unit Price.

Doing breakeven analysis calculations can be facilitated by the use of a breakeven formatted income statement. This is an income statement that has costs reformatted into variable costs and fixed costs.

Cash Flow Budget

Having a cash flow budget is the first step in getting control of your cash flow and creating a cash flow budget is a basic part of business planning. It is a projection of cash inflows and outflows that allows you to plan cash balances in advance, reducing unpleasant cash surprises, and minimizing the chances you will have to borrow money or factor receivables to raise cash to cover expenses. Cash flow budgets are typically created monthly, but can be created weekly or even daily.

Efficiency Ratios

Your business has finite resources. You will need to use them efficiently to manage your cash flow and control costs. Resource use has an effect on cost competitiveness. The four ratios below will help you do that.

Accounts Receivable to Sales Ratio - Accounts receivable is uncollected money from sales made on credit to your customers. The accounts receivable to sales ratio looks at the ratio of uncollected receivables in comparison to your sales. Keeping track of this ratio will help identify problems with cash collections. Problems with cash collections could indicate future cash flow problems for your business.

The way to calculate this ratio is

Accounts Receivable / Monthly Sales = Accounts Receivable to Sales Ratio.

Average Collection Period - This ratio, also known as the Days Sales Outstanding, measures the length of time it takes to turn sales into cash. In other words, the average number of days to collect from your customers. The amount in your accounts receivable can be converted to the number of days sales outstanding. The longer the time, the more you have invested in accounts receivable. The way to calculate average collection period is

Current Accounts Receivable Balance / (Annual Sales / 360) = Average Collection Period.

Inventory to Sales Ratio - Your inventory supports your sales and as such, should have a fairly constant relationship to one another. The formula to calculate this ratio is

Inventory / Monthly Net Sales = Inventory to Sales Ratio.

If sales increase, then inventory should increase a similar percentage. The increase in inventory to support the added sales may be an issue from a cash flow perspective as you would need to pay for it, but from an operational perspective it doesn't seem unreasonable, assuming the inventory was in line in the first place.

Average Days of Inventory on Hand - Your business has inventory to support sales. As such, your inventory investment will support your sales for a period of time and then run out. Therefore, the dollars you have invested in inventory can be converted to days of inventory on hand before it is sold. The longer the days of inventory on hand, the greater the investment in inventory required and the greater the pressure on cash flow. The way you measure average days of inventory on hand is

Current Inventory / (Annual Cost of Goods Sold / 360) = Average Days Inventory on Hand.

Income Statement

The income statement is a summary of transactions over a specific accounting period, typically a month, a quarter or a year. It's also commonly referred to as the P&L. Essentially it is revenue minus expenses equal a profit or a loss. Again, profit does not equal cash. Revenue is recognized when a sale is made, which is typically on credit, or terms. Cash is collected later when your customer pays their invoice. Product is manufactured or merchandise purchased and put into inventory, and is not recognized as cost of goods sold expense until the product or merchandise is sold. Merchandise for resale or materials used in the manufacture of goods going into inventory are charged to accounts payable and cash is paid later when the payable is due.

Income statement information can also be constructed to allow the side by side comparison of income statements over sequential periods of time. Besides comparing the actual numbers over time, it can also be helpful if you compare percentages such as percent of cost of goods sold to sales, gross profit to sales or operating costs to sales. These can be very useful in determining how your business is trending.

Key Performance Indicators or Key Success Indicators

Some measurements of your business are key to your business's success. When you have decided on a group of metrics tied to specific targets that are key to your business's success, and are under your control and actionable, you have what are called Key Performance Indicators (KPI) or Key Success Indicators.

These metrics can differ throughout the organization. For instance, at the general management level there might be measurements and targets at a very high level such as sales investments in accounts receivable and inventory, current ratio, fixed costs as a percent of sales, and gross profit margin. If the measurement was for manufacturing or operations, then metrics and targets about product cycle time, time per service call, reject rates or percent of orders shipped complete might be in order. A customer service department KPI might be the number of calls answered within one minute against a targeted level of performance.

Notice that in each case, the measurement is quantifiable, is associated with a performance level target and can be influenced by management action. If you can't measure it numerically, or do anything about it or as a result of it, then in most cases keeping track of it serves no purpose.

Your group of KPIs should be relatively small to focus attention on what is important and then be organized in a way that they can be viewed conveniently on one report. This report is called a scorecard or dashboard.

Liquidity Ratios

Liquidity ratios generally indicate your business's ability to quickly raise cash to pay bills. They are important as a problem revealed by one of these ratios could mean you are at risk of not being able to meet your short-term obligations. For this reason, creditors and bankers often pay particularly close attention to these ratios. Below are two liquidity ratios.

Current Ratio - Probably the most commonly used ratio of any of the balance sheet ratios is the current ratio. It is the ratio of current assets to current liabilities and generally indicates your business's ability to generate enough cash to pay its bills. The formula is

Current Assets / Current Liabilities = Current Ratio.

Although the number can vary by industry and situation, a good rule of thumb is a current ratio of 2:1 or better, that is your current assets are at least twice your current liabilities. If you start to see a decrease in this ratio, it could either be a decrease in current assets, or an increase in short-term debt and payables. In any event, a decrease indicates a reduced ability to generate enough cash to pay short-term obligations.

Quick or Acid Test Ratio - This ratio is similar in purpose to the current ratio. However, one of the problems with the current ratio is that it includes all current assets as an indication of your business's ability to pay current obligations. This includes inventory and pre-paid expenses. However, inventory has to be sold to be turned into cash, which may or may not be possible to do quickly. Pre-paid expenses can't be turned into cash at all. The quick ratio (or acid test ratio) eliminates these current assets to more accurately assess your business's ability to generate cash to pay current bills. This modification of current assets is called quick current assets. The formula for the quick ratio is

Current Assets - (inventory + prepaid expenses) / Current Liabilities = Quick Ratio.

Again, the number can vary by industry or situation, but a good rule of thumb is a quick ratio of 1:1 or better, that is the quick current assets are at least as much as current liabilities. .

Marketing Plan

There are a lot of things that go into a marketing plan. Two of the things the plan should include are the goals for the advertising and marketing, and a budget. The goals of your advertising and marketing plan should include what it's trying to accomplish in terms of brand awareness, brand positioning or sales increases. Before you develop any marketing collateral, material or activities, there should be well defined and measurable goals.

In order to project the effect of your advertising and marketing, you will also need a budget. This will define the cost part of the cost benefit equation. Once you have a budget, a desired outcome and some other metrics like conversion rates, you can start to calculate whether the likely benefit is worth the proposed cost.

Profitability Ratios

There are ways to measure your business's profitability from the information in the income statement and balance sheet. These are ratios and percentages comparing one number in the income statement to another number in the income statement, or one number in the income statement to another number in the balance sheet. The reason that ratios and percentages are useful is that they put the numbers in context.

There are three profitability ratios that measure some form of profit against sales. The ratios are designed to measure how much of your sales is turning into profit. There are two more ratios that measure profit against assets and owner's equity. They are measures of how well your business has done with the resources committed to its operation.

The five ratios below are profitability ratios.

Return on Assets - This ratio, also known as ROA, measures how effectively your business is using its assets to produce profit. Although not a measure that can be managed directly, it does measure the relative performance of the assets employed and as such, will tell a story over time. The calculation for return on assets is

Net Income / Total Assets = Return on Assets expressed as a percent.

Good ROA ratios vary by industry and situation. Industries with large asset requirements such as manufacturing and transportation might aim at 5% while software and service firms might aim at 20% or more.

Return on Equity - Sometimes called return on investment or ROI, the return on equity ratio measures the return in the form of profits generated by your investment in the business. As such, your business's ROI should exceed what you could have earned in a substitute investment such as stocks, bonds, CDs or income producing real estate. This ratio measures how effectively you have invested your money.

The calculation for ROI is

Net Income / Owner's Equity = ROI.

As a general rule of thumb, a good ROI is more than 20%.

Gross Margin Percentage - Gross profit is sales minus cost of goods sold. The gross margin percentage is gross profit as a percent of sales. If the percentage is decreasing, it may mean that increases in your costs are outstripping your increases in pricing.

Gross margin percentage is calculated as

Gross Profit / Sales = Gross Profit Margin Percentage.

Operating Profit Percentage - Operating profit is calculated as gross profit minus operating expenses. The operating profit percentage has all the same issues as the gross profit percentage, plus the addition of fixed costs into the equation. If the percentage is decreasing, is there a problem with your gross margin? Are your fixed costs getting out of line?

Operating profit percentage is calculated as

Operating Profit / Sales = Operating Profit Percentage.

As an aside, although not strictly a profitability ratio, the **percentage of operating expense to sales** is a way to keep tabs on the efficiency of your operating expenses. If the percentage is increasing, this may indicate a problem as your fixed costs are increasing at a faster rate than your sales. This percentage can be calculated as

Operating Expenses / Sales = Percentage of Operating Expenses to Sales.

<u>Net Income Percentage</u> is calculated the same way as the others and tracks your bottom line. Remember that net income is calculated as operating income minus interest expense and taxes (if applicable). So net income percentage is calculated as

Net Income / Sales = Net Income Percentage.

Profit Projection and Profit Modeling

Similar to breakeven analysis, profit projection and profit modeling use the same formulas to project profits under varying sets of circumstances. Instead of dividing fixed costs by the contribution margin percent to get a breakeven point, profit projection multiplies sales by the contribution margin percent to get a contribution margin and then subtracts fixed costs from the contribution margin to project a profit. This can be expressed as

(Sales * Contribution Margin percent) - Fixed Costs = Profit.

Profit projection can be useful in making pricing, investment and marketing decisions because it allows you to project what the possible results of your decision might be, lessening the chance of a costly mistake.

SMART Goals

SMART is an acronym for Specific, Measurable, Actionable, Realistic and Time bound. It's a way of thinking about goals with some specificity, since the goals need to meet the five criteria of SMART. The goals should be specific and not general, progress and success need to be measurable, they should point to specific action, the goals have to be realistic and believable, and they must have a deadline.

Solvency Ratios

Solvency ratios are a set of ratios that measure your business's financial risk. In this case, your ability to pay debt obligations regardless of cash flow. Generally this means the less debt the better. Below are two ratios that measure the financial risk that debt is posing to your business.

<u>Debt to Equity</u> - The debt to equity ratio measures your business's leverage employed to increase profitability. Debt in this case means borrowing and is expressed as total debt. These debts are compared with owner's equity to create a ratio. The formula is

Total Debt / Owner's Equity = Debt to Equity Ratio.

Too large a debt burden may increase leverage and improve profitability, but too much debt may become too much for your business to handle and lead to bankruptcy. The lower this ratio, the less financial risk to your business.

<u>Debt to Assets</u> - This ratio shows how much of your business is financed by creditors. The formula for this is

Total Debt / Total Assets = Debt to Asset Ratio expressed as a percent.

As with other ratios, the number may vary by industry and situation, but a good rule of thumb is to have a debt to assets ratio of below 50%. Higher than that may indicate you have too much debt creating the possible risk of the your inability to pay it.

Statement of Cash Flows

The statement of cash flows (also known as a cash flow statement) shows the sources and uses of cash in your business and is for the same period of time as the income statement such as a month, a quarter or a year. It shows changes in cash from operations, investment activities and financing activities. Sources of cash can be operations, new loans, issuing stock or sale of plant and equipment. Uses of cash can be operations, dividends, loan repayment, stock repurchase or purchase of plant and equipment. There are three sections to the statement of cash flows: They are cash from operations, cash from investing activities and cash from financing activities.

The formula for cash flow can be expressed as

Profit
+ **Depreciation/Amortization (cash from operations) (add back non-cash expense)**
± **Inventory change (cash from operations) (inventory increase means cash decrease)**
± **Accounts Receivable change (cash from operations) (accounts receivable increase means cash decrease)**
± **Accounts Payable change (cash from operations) (accounts payable increase means cash increase)**
± **Fixed Asset change (cash from investing activities) (fixed asset increase means cash decrease)**
± **Debt Obligations (cash from financing activities) (debt increase means cash increase)**
= **Cash Flow**

Profitability Thinking

About John Bulman, MBA

John Bulman is a business coach and trainer who combines financial acumen with a background in financial management, sales management and supply chain management to create business performance solutions using key metrics to define process improvements. He does this by breaking down issues into discreet components, identifying issues with them, and creating and teaching effective, simple and easy to implement solutions to improve business performance. He has a unique talent for deciphering complex financial and operational matters, and explaining them in a way a layman can easily understand.

Having a diverse career path has led John to create business solutions in the financial service, manufacturing and distribution industries. He has held management level positions and been a key staff member in each of these areas. In each role, he has strategically coached, mentored and led business units to improved profitability and performance. These improvements included changes in sales culture and processes that led to dramatically improved revenues, sales volume, marketing, efficiency and profitability, as well as improvements in manufacturing and distribution processes that led to significantly reduced costs, lead times and inventory investments, as well as improved customer satisfaction.

Because of his performance, unique skill set and ability to develop people that transcends markets, John is a sought after resource with managers and senior executives from across the nation interested in his perspectives, guidance and expertise. He believes that if you can change a team's skills and thinking at the same time, amazing results can happen. Everything John has done in each of his roles has been designed to accomplish that.

Creating and leading seminars about understanding business and financial models, break even analysis, creating return-on-investment, sales process improvement, sales management, creating business plans, creating business processes that work, collapsing supply chains to improve performance, and leadership, John understands the challenges in today's business environment and how to overcome them. His passion is working one-on-one with clients to improve performance in their businesses.

John holds a MBA from the Illinois Institute of Technology - Stuart School in Chicago as well as a BA from National-Louis University. He is married and lives in Mission Viejo, California. John Bulman can be reached at jb@profitabilitythinking.com.

Made in the USA
Columbia, SC
27 April 2018